Feature Engineering and Model Tuning: Practical Data Science Techniques:

James Relington

DEDICATION

To those who seek knowledge, inspiration, and new perspectives—
may this book be a companion on your journey, a spark for curiosity,
and a reminder that every page turned is a step toward discovery.

Foundations of Feature Engineering in Data Science 8

Understanding Raw Data and Its Limitations 11

Feature Selection vs Feature Extraction 14

Dealing with Missing Data for Reliable Features 17

Handling Outliers in Feature Engineering 20

Encoding Categorical Variables for Modeling 23

Numerical Feature Transformation Techniques 27

Binning and Discretization Strategies 30

Scaling and Normalization for Consistent Features 33

Text Feature Engineering Using NLP Techniques 37

Vectorizing Text with Count and TF-IDF 40

Feature Engineering for Time Series Data 44

Lag Features and Rolling Statistics 47

Cyclical Encoding of Time-based Variables 50

Feature Engineering from Dates and Timestamps 53

Extracting Features from Images 56

Audio and Signal Processing for Feature Creation 60

Feature Engineering in Graph-Based Data 63

Dimensionality Reduction with PCA 67

Feature Selection Using Filter Methods 70

Wrapper Methods for Feature Selection 73

Embedded Methods for Feature Relevance 76

Mutual Information and Correlation Analysis 79

Dealing with Multicollinearity in Features 83

Creating Interaction Features for Nonlinear Models 86

Polynomial Feature Generation 89

Target Encoding for High-Cardinality Variables 93

Hashing Tricks and Memory-Efficient Representations 96

Domain Knowledge in Feature Engineering 99

Feature Engineering in E-Commerce Data 102

Handling Imbalanced Data through Feature Design 106

Feature Engineering for Recommender Systems 109

Engineering Features for Fraud Detection 113

Feature Engineering for Medical and Genomic Data 116

Model Tuning Fundamentals 120

Hyperparameter Tuning with Grid Search 123

Random Search for Hyperparameter Optimization 127

Bayesian Optimization for Model Tuning 130

Tuning Decision Trees and Random Forests 133

Regularization Techniques in Linear Models 137

Tuning Gradient Boosted Trees 140

Hyperparameter Tuning in Neural Networks 143

Dropout, Batch Normalization, and Learning Rate Schedules 146

Cross-Validation Strategies for Reliable Tuning 150

Early Stopping and Model Convergence 153

Automated Machine Learning and Feature Engineering 156

Feature Importance Metrics in Tree Models 160

SHAP and LIME for Model Interpretability 163

Feature Drift Detection and Updating 166

Feature Engineering in Production Pipelines 170

Scalable Feature Engineering with Big Data Tools 173

Continuous Tuning and Monitoring in Production 177

AKNOWLEDGEMENTS

I would like to express my deepest gratitude to everyone who contributed to the creation of this book. To my colleagues and mentors, your insights and expertise have been invaluable. A special thank you to my family and friends for their unwavering support and encouragement throughout this journey.

Foundations of Feature Engineering in Data Science

Feature engineering is the cornerstone of practical data science. It refers to the process of transforming raw data into meaningful representations that can be effectively used by machine learning models. Despite the increasing power and accessibility of modern algorithms, the performance of any data-driven solution remains heavily dependent on the quality of the features used. Strong feature engineering can compensate for a mediocre model, while poor features can make even the most advanced algorithms fail. It is through the design, selection, and transformation of features that data is shaped into a format that reveals the patterns, relationships, and signals needed for accurate predictions.

At the heart of feature engineering lies the understanding that raw data, in its original form, is rarely suitable for direct use in modeling. Real-world datasets often contain inconsistencies, missing values, noise, and variables that require transformation to uncover their predictive power. The first step in any feature engineering effort is gaining a deep understanding of the dataset. This includes inspecting data types, summarizing statistics, visualizing distributions, and identifying the nature of each variable. Categorical variables might hold embedded hierarchies or latent information, while numerical values might follow non-linear trends or be influenced by external factors such as time, geography, or user behavior.

One of the most powerful aspects of feature engineering is its ability to inject domain knowledge into the modeling process. Data scientists can use their understanding of the problem context to create new variables that reflect business rules, operational conditions, or behavioral patterns. For example, in an e-commerce dataset, raw transaction logs may be converted into customer lifetime value estimates, average basket size, or time since last purchase. These features are not directly available in the raw data but can be derived from it using a combination of logic, statistical techniques, and contextual insight. By encoding these ideas into the feature space, models are provided with structured access to domain-relevant information that can significantly enhance predictive performance.

Transformations of existing features play a crucial role in making data suitable for machine learning algorithms. Many models assume that input features are normally distributed, independent, or lie within a certain range. Transformations such as log scaling, square root, or Box-Cox can help normalize skewed distributions. Standardization and normalization bring different features onto a common scale, preventing features with larger magnitudes from dominating the learning process. This is especially important for algorithms that rely on distance metrics, such as k-nearest neighbors or support vector machines, where differences in feature scales can distort the geometry of the input space.

Feature encoding is another foundational aspect of the engineering process, particularly for categorical data. Algorithms require numerical inputs, so non-numeric categories must be transformed into numerical representations. This can be done through label encoding, one-hot encoding, binary encoding, or more advanced techniques like target encoding and embeddings. Each method comes with trade-offs in terms of information preservation, model complexity, and overfitting risk. For instance, one-hot encoding is simple and preserves category uniqueness but can lead to high-dimensional datasets when applied to variables with many distinct values. In contrast, target encoding captures category-level trends with respect to the target variable but introduces the risk of target leakage if not handled carefully.

The challenge of missing data also arises frequently in feature engineering. Missing values can result from data entry errors, system issues, or inherent characteristics of the dataset. How these values are handled can dramatically influence model behavior. Imputation strategies, such as mean or median filling, k-nearest neighbors imputation, or more sophisticated model-based approaches, help to preserve dataset integrity while minimizing bias. In some cases, the absence of a value can itself be informative, and creating a binary indicator for missingness can add predictive value.

Another key concept is the identification and treatment of outliers. Outliers can distort distributions, skew model parameters, and lead to erroneous conclusions. Detecting outliers through statistical thresholds, clustering techniques, or distance-based methods allows data scientists to decide whether to remove, transform, or isolate these anomalies. In certain domains, such as fraud detection or industrial fault monitoring, outliers may be precisely the data points of interest, requiring thoughtful engineering to capture their unique characteristics.

The iterative nature of feature engineering is vital to understand. It is rarely a linear process. Instead, it involves cycles of hypothesis, transformation, evaluation, and refinement. As models are trained and their performance analyzed, insights about feature importance, correlation, redundancy, and interaction effects emerge. These insights, in turn, guide further engineering. Tools such as permutation importance, SHAP values, and partial dependence plots help illuminate the relationships between features and predictions, supporting the creation of new derived features or the elimination of unhelpful ones.

Feature engineering is deeply connected to the nature of the model being used. Different models have different sensitivities and preferences when it comes to features. Linear models benefit from well-scaled, independent variables and are limited in capturing non-linear relationships unless interactions or polynomial terms are included. Tree-based models like random forests and gradient boosting can automatically handle non-linearity and interactions but may require careful treatment of missing values and high-cardinality categorical variables. Neural networks thrive with large feature sets and unstructured inputs but require rigorous normalization and benefit from learned embeddings for categorical data.

Ultimately, feature engineering is both an art and a science. It requires a blend of creativity, domain expertise, and technical skill. While automated machine learning systems and deep learning architectures have shifted some of the burden away from manual feature crafting, the importance of understanding how to shape data into effective representations remains undiminished. The foundations laid through robust feature engineering not only improve model accuracy but also enhance interpretability, fairness, and generalizability. The process of turning raw, messy data into a refined, insightful set of features is one of the most impactful contributions a data scientist can make to any project.

Understanding Raw Data and Its Limitations

Before any effective data science or machine learning process can begin, it is crucial to thoroughly understand the raw data. Raw data is the untouched, original form of data collected from various sources such as databases, sensors, user interactions, transactions, social media platforms, or logs. While it represents the starting point for any analytical task, raw data is rarely clean, complete, or ready for immediate use. It often contains inconsistencies, errors, redundancies, and other issues that, if not addressed, can significantly hinder the performance of models and lead to misleading results. Understanding the structure, content, and limitations of raw data is a foundational step in the feature engineering process.

Raw data is typically messy and unstructured or semi-structured, depending on the source. It may arrive in tabular format, JSON records, XML documents, audio files, image formats, or even as plain text. Regardless of the format, raw data often lacks the organization required for analytical processing. It may contain duplicate entries, inconsistent naming conventions, malformed records, or embedded noise. For instance, in a customer database, one might find the same person registered under slightly different names or with different formatting of the same address. These seemingly minor inconsistencies can lead to serious aggregation errors and flawed insights if left uncorrected.

A key limitation of raw data is the prevalence of missing values. These gaps can arise from a variety of causes, including user non-responses, sensor malfunctions, system glitches, or data corruption during transmission. The presence of missing values can have far-reaching effects on data quality. Many machine learning algorithms cannot handle missing data directly, and naive imputation techniques can introduce bias or noise. It is therefore essential to determine whether the missingness is random or if it follows a pattern that may itself carry informative signals. For example, in a medical dataset, missing lab results might be correlated with a patient not undergoing certain tests due to financial constraints, which could in turn be predictive of other health outcomes.

Noise is another common issue in raw data. Noise refers to irrelevant or meaningless information that obscures the underlying signal. This can be seen in text data as typographical errors, in numerical data as random measurement errors, or in images as pixel artifacts. Separating signal from noise is one of the central challenges in data science, and doing so requires a solid understanding of the data's origin, context, and intended use. Excessive noise can weaken models, increase overfitting, and reduce interpretability. Detecting and mitigating noise is a delicate task that must balance cleaning the data while preserving valuable variation.

Raw data is also often unbalanced and biased. This is especially true in domains like fraud detection, medical diagnostics, and recommendation systems. For instance, in fraud detection, the majority of transactions are legitimate, and fraudulent events make up a very small percentage of the data. This imbalance can result in models that simply learn to predict the majority class, achieving high accuracy while failing to detect the minority class altogether. Similarly, biases in data collection can reflect systemic inequalities or flaws in the way data is gathered. If not identified and corrected, these biases can be amplified by models, leading to unethical or inaccurate outcomes.

A critical part of understanding raw data involves exploratory data analysis. This process includes summarizing the data with statistics, visualizing distributions, inspecting correlations, and identifying anomalies. These steps help in forming hypotheses about the data and uncovering patterns that may not be immediately visible. For example, histograms can reveal skewness in numerical variables, scatter plots can expose outliers, and correlation matrices can indicate multicollinearity. These insights guide the decisions on how to engineer features that better capture the data's true structure and relationships.

Categorical variables in raw data often present their own challenges. These may be stored as strings with inconsistent capitalization, unexpected symbols, or embedded codes. A column that appears to contain country names might include values like USA, U.S., United States, or even null values, all referring to the same entity. Without cleaning and standardizing such values, any analysis based on them would be unreliable. Moreover, some categorical variables may have a high cardinality, meaning they include a vast number of unique values. This can create challenges for encoding methods and may introduce sparsity or overfitting in models unless handled carefully.

Temporal data introduces further complexity. Raw timestamps may come in different formats, contain time zone inconsistencies, or include missing components such as seconds or milliseconds. Time-based features often require special parsing and formatting to ensure consistency. Furthermore, when working with time series, one must consider lag effects, seasonality, and trends that are not immediately apparent in the raw form. Ignoring these temporal dependencies can lead to models that overlook crucial patterns or violate assumptions about data independence.

The origin of the data is also a critical factor. Data collected manually is more prone to human error, while data from sensors might suffer from drift or calibration issues. Data extracted from APIs can change structure over time due to updates, which introduces instability. Understanding how the data was collected, stored, and processed provides necessary context for evaluating its reliability and consistency. Without this context, it is easy to misinterpret what the data actually represents.

Understanding raw data also means recognizing its boundaries. No dataset captures the entire reality. There are always factors not included in the data that might affect the outcome. This limitation must be acknowledged when modeling and drawing conclusions. Overconfidence in the representativeness of raw data can lead to overfitting and poor generalization when models are deployed in real-world scenarios.

Ultimately, understanding raw data is not a one-time task but an ongoing process throughout the life cycle of a data science project. As new insights emerge and models evolve, the interpretation of the data may shift. New patterns might come to light, or previously ignored variables may become relevant. Data scientists must maintain a critical and curious mindset, constantly questioning the data and its limitations, and be ready to revisit earlier assumptions as new evidence presents itself. By thoroughly understanding raw data, data scientists lay the groundwork for effective feature engineering, robust modeling, and reliable decision-making.

Feature Selection vs Feature Extraction

In the world of data science and machine learning, the quality and relevance of features used in a model often determine its success. As datasets grow in complexity and size, it becomes increasingly important to manage the feature space effectively. Two fundamental strategies used to enhance the usefulness of features are feature selection and feature extraction. Although both aim to improve model performance and reduce computational burden, they operate in fundamentally different ways and serve distinct purposes within the feature engineering process.

Feature selection focuses on identifying and retaining only the most relevant features from the original dataset. It is a process of pruning, where the goal is to eliminate features that are redundant, irrelevant, or noisy. This is achieved by analyzing each feature's contribution to the target variable, either through statistical tests, correlation metrics, or through its impact on model performance. The central idea is that not all features provide meaningful information. Some may offer no predictive value, while others may introduce noise, multicollinearity, or unnecessary complexity that ultimately degrades model performance. By selecting only the most impactful features, data scientists can simplify models, enhance generalization, and make interpretations more straightforward.

In contrast, feature extraction transforms the original features into a new set of variables through mathematical or algorithmic techniques. Rather than selecting from the existing variables, it creates new ones, often in a lower-dimensional space. These new features are designed to capture the most essential aspects of the data while discarding noise and irrelevant variation. A classic example is Principal Component Analysis, where linear combinations of the original variables are used to form a set of orthogonal components. These components retain the most variance in the data and provide a compact representation. Feature extraction is especially useful when dealing with high-dimensional data, such as images, text, or gene sequences, where the raw features are too numerous or sparse to model directly.

The choice between feature selection and feature extraction is influenced by several factors, including the nature of the data, the objectives of the analysis, and the interpretability requirements. When interpretability is crucial, feature selection is often preferred because it retains the original variables, making it easier to understand and explain the model's decisions. For example, in medical diagnostics or financial modeling, stakeholders may demand to know which specific factors influenced a prediction. Feature extraction, by contrast, creates new composite variables that may be mathematically meaningful but are less intuitive. This trade-off between performance and transparency must be carefully balanced, especially in regulated industries or high-stakes decision-making.

Feature selection can be implemented using various techniques that fall into three main categories: filter methods, wrapper methods, and embedded methods. Filter methods rely on statistical properties of the data, such as correlation coefficients, mutual information, or chi-squared statistics, to rank and choose features independently of any specific model. These methods are fast and scalable but may overlook interactions between features. Wrapper methods, on the other hand, evaluate subsets of features by training and testing models, iteratively searching for combinations that yield the best performance. While more accurate, they are computationally intensive and prone to overfitting on small datasets. Embedded methods incorporate feature selection directly into the model training process. Techniques like Lasso regression, decision tree pruning, and regularization are examples where the model itself penalizes or discards less useful features.

Feature extraction methods, in contrast, are generally more mathematical in nature. Dimensionality reduction techniques like PCA, t-SNE, and UMAP are widely used to reduce complexity while preserving the underlying structure of the data. These methods can uncover latent patterns and groupings that are not visible in the original feature space. In deep learning, feature extraction often takes the form of learned representations. For instance, convolutional neural networks automatically extract hierarchical features from images, moving from raw pixel data to high-level abstractions such as shapes and objects. Similarly, word embeddings in natural language processing transform sparse text data into dense vector representations that capture semantic relationships between words and phrases.

One of the key challenges in both feature selection and feature extraction is avoiding the loss of critical information. Aggressively reducing the number of features without considering the impact on model performance can lead to underfitting and poor generalization. It is essential to evaluate the effect of these processes not only on model accuracy but also on robustness and consistency across different data splits and scenarios. Cross-validation, permutation tests, and performance metrics must be used rigorously to ensure that the reduced feature set still captures the essence of the problem.

Scalability is another important consideration. As datasets become larger and more complex, especially in big data environments, the ability to efficiently select or extract features becomes vital. Feature selection techniques that are computationally lightweight are better suited for real-time applications, while more resource-intensive feature extraction methods may require batch processing or specialized hardware acceleration. The infrastructure and processing capabilities of the environment must be aligned with the chosen approach.

The impact of feature selection and extraction extends beyond model training. In deployment, a leaner feature set reduces the memory footprint, speeds up predictions, and simplifies maintenance. This is particularly valuable in edge computing scenarios, where models must operate on devices with limited resources. Furthermore, by reducing the dimensionality of the data, these techniques help mitigate the curse of dimensionality, where the volume of the feature space grows so large that data points become sparse and distance metrics lose meaning.

Ultimately, feature selection and feature extraction are not mutually exclusive. In practice, they are often used in combination. A data scientist may begin with feature selection to eliminate irrelevant or redundant features and then apply feature extraction to the remaining set to capture deeper patterns or reduce dimensionality further. The art lies in knowing when to use each technique and how to adapt them to the specific characteristics of the data and the goals of the analysis. Mastery of these techniques allows practitioners to build models that are not only more accurate but also more efficient, interpretable, and adaptable to changing conditions. Understanding the nuances of these approaches is essential for any data scientist seeking to extract real value from raw information.

Dealing with Missing Data for Reliable Features

In real-world datasets, missing data is an inevitable challenge that can significantly impact the quality of machine learning models. It is rarely the case that data collected from diverse sources, such as sensors, databases, or user inputs, comes in a perfect and complete form. Missing values can arise for a variety of reasons, including human error, data corruption, or the inherent nature of the data collection process. Addressing missing data effectively is crucial, as improper handling can lead to biased models, reduced accuracy, and unreliable predictions. How one deals with missing data determines the integrity and reliability of the features used in machine learning models.

The first step in addressing missing data is understanding why the data is missing. Not all missingness is created equal, and categorizing the missing data can help inform the best strategy for handling it. Missing data can be classified into three types: missing completely at random (MCAR), missing at random (MAR), and missing not at random (MNAR). MCAR refers to missing values that have no relationship with any other observed or unobserved variables in the dataset. In such cases, the missingness does not introduce any bias, and the data can often be safely ignored or imputed without affecting model performance. MAR occurs when the missingness is related to some observed data but not the unobserved data, meaning that the pattern of missingness can be explained by other variables. Finally, MNAR refers to situations where the missingness is related to the unobserved data itself, which can introduce bias into the model if not handled carefully. Understanding the underlying mechanism of missing data helps guide the choice of imputation or modeling techniques.

Handling missing data requires careful consideration of both the quantity and the distribution of the missing values. If the proportion of missing data is small and distributed randomly across the dataset, one may decide to ignore the missing values without significantly affecting the analysis. In other cases, however, where missing data is substantial or correlated with other variables, the approach to handling it becomes more complex. Simply removing rows with missing values can lead to a loss of valuable information and introduce bias, especially in cases where the missingness is not random. As a result, imputation methods are often employed to fill in missing values and preserve the integrity of the dataset.

One of the most common techniques for dealing with missing data is imputation, where missing values are replaced with substituted values based on the observed data. The simplest form of imputation is mean or median imputation, where the missing value is replaced by the mean or median of the observed values for that feature. While this method is computationally efficient, it can introduce bias if the data is not normally distributed or if there are outliers that distort the mean. Moreover, mean or median imputation does not account for potential relationships between features, which could result in a loss of variability and the introduction of unrealistic correlations. A more sophisticated approach is k-nearest neighbors (KNN) imputation, where missing values are predicted based on the values of the nearest data points. KNN imputation is particularly useful when there are strong relationships between features, but it can be computationally expensive for large datasets.

Another popular method of imputation is regression imputation, where the missing values are predicted using a regression model built from the non-missing data. This approach allows for more flexibility, as it can account for the relationships between the feature with missing values and other features. However, regression imputation assumes a linear relationship between features, which may not always be the case. More advanced techniques such as multiple imputation and Bayesian imputation involve generating multiple plausible values for the missing data and using them in combination to estimate the uncertainty in the imputed values. These methods are more computationally intensive but can provide a more accurate representation of the missing data and account for the uncertainty introduced by imputation.

When dealing with missing categorical data, the strategies may differ slightly. In some cases, the missing value can be imputed with the most frequent category, which is a simple approach that works well when the categorical variable has a high frequency of one particular value. However, this method can introduce bias if the missingness is not random or if the missing category is important for predictive modeling. Alternatively, categorical imputation can involve using the mode, or more advanced techniques like KNN imputation, where missing categories are imputed based on the closest neighbors. For more complex datasets, one might employ machine learning algorithms specifically designed to handle missing categorical values, such as decision trees or random forests, which can predict missing categories based on patterns in other features.

While imputation can restore the dataset's integrity, it is not always the best solution, especially when the missing data is extensive or the missingness is systematically related to other variables. In such cases, a more advanced approach may involve using models that can handle missing data directly. Decision trees, random forests, and gradient boosting machines are examples of models that can accommodate missing values without the need for imputation. These models are capable of splitting data on features even when some values are missing, allowing them to make predictions without losing valuable information. However, relying on such models may not always be appropriate, particularly if the missingness is heavily biased or if it significantly distorts the data distribution.

In some cases, it may be useful to create a feature indicating whether a value is missing. This approach, known as missingness encoding, treats the presence of missing values as a signal in itself. For example, in a medical dataset, the absence of a value for a particular test might indicate that the patient did not receive the test, which could carry important predictive information. By encoding the missingness as a separate binary feature, the model can learn to differentiate between cases where data is absent due to a lack of information versus cases where the absence itself is meaningful.

The treatment of missing data is not a one-size-fits-all process; it requires a thorough understanding of the dataset and the domain context. The key to effective handling lies in assessing the impact of missing data on the model and choosing an appropriate technique that preserves the data's integrity without introducing bias. By carefully considering the mechanisms behind the missingness, the type of data being dealt with, and the relationships between features, one can ensure that missing data is handled in a way that maintains the reliability and accuracy of the resulting machine learning models.

Handling Outliers in Feature Engineering

Outliers are data points that deviate significantly from the majority of observations in a dataset. They may appear as unusually high or low values and can occur in both numerical and categorical variables. In the context of feature engineering, handling outliers is a critical task, as these extreme values can distort statistical summaries, mislead learning algorithms, and ultimately compromise the performance and generalizability of machine learning models. Understanding the origin, nature, and potential impact of outliers is essential for designing features that capture meaningful patterns without being overwhelmed by noise or anomalies.

Outliers can arise from various sources. Some are the result of genuine variability in the data, reflecting rare but valid events. Others may be caused by data entry errors, measurement inaccuracies, or issues during data transmission and storage. In financial data, for instance, an unusually large transaction might be the result of fraud, a system glitch, or simply a legitimate purchase. In medical records, outliers could indicate a serious health condition, a misreported measurement, or an edge case that defies the typical clinical profile. The challenge lies in determining whether an outlier should be removed, transformed, or preserved. This decision should be guided by domain knowledge, statistical analysis, and the intended use of the data.

Identifying outliers is the first step in handling them. Several statistical techniques are commonly used for detection. One of the most basic methods involves using summary statistics such as the mean and standard deviation. In a normal distribution, data points that fall more than a certain number of standard deviations away from the mean can be considered outliers. However, this approach assumes symmetry and can be heavily influenced by the very outliers it seeks to detect. A more robust alternative is the interquartile range method, which defines outliers as observations lying beyond 1.5 times the interquartile range above the third quartile or below the first quartile. This method is less sensitive to extreme values and works well for skewed distributions.

Visualization also plays an important role in spotting outliers. Box plots, scatter plots, and histograms allow data scientists to see where data points cluster and where anomalies occur. These visual tools are especially useful for multivariate analysis, where an outlier in one dimension may not stand out until viewed in the context of other variables. In higher-dimensional spaces, techniques such as Mahalanobis distance, isolation forests, and clustering algorithms can be employed to identify points that are dissimilar to the rest of the dataset. These advanced methods consider the overall structure of the data and are better suited for complex, non-linear relationships.

Once outliers have been identified, the next step is deciding how to handle them. In some cases, it may be appropriate to remove outliers altogether, especially when they are clearly the result of data corruption or entry errors. Eliminating such anomalies can improve the consistency of the dataset and reduce the risk of misleading the model. However, removing outliers indiscriminately can be dangerous, particularly if those values represent valid but rare events. In fraud detection, for example, the outliers may be precisely the instances that the model needs to learn from. Deleting them would weaken the model's ability to detect future fraudulent behavior.

Transforming outliers is another common strategy. Applying logarithmic, square root, or Box-Cox transformations can compress extreme values and bring them closer to the bulk of the distribution. These transformations are useful when outliers skew the distribution of a feature, potentially violating the assumptions of certain algorithms. For instance, linear regression models assume normally distributed residuals, and severe outliers can distort the model's coefficients. By transforming the data, one can mitigate these effects and allow the model to capture the underlying relationships more accurately.

Another approach involves capping or flooring the outliers, also known as winsorizing. This method limits the extreme values to a certain percentile, such as the 1st and 99th percentiles, thereby reducing their influence without completely discarding them. Capping can be particularly effective in situations where extreme values are expected but should not disproportionately affect the model. For example, in pricing data, a few very high prices might dominate the scale and obscure trends in the more common price ranges. By capping these values, the model can focus on the central distribution while still accounting for the presence of outliers.

Binning is another technique that can help in managing outliers. Instead of treating a variable as continuous, it can be divided into intervals or categories, with each bin representing a range of values. This can simplify the treatment of extreme values by placing them into broader categories and reducing their impact on the model. Binning also makes sense when the data is naturally grouped into levels or ranges, such as age groups or income brackets. However, care must be taken to ensure that binning does not eliminate useful variation or mask important trends in the data.

In many cases, the presence of outliers can be informative and should be preserved. Outliers may represent important edge cases, emerging trends, or warning signs. Rather than suppressing them, data scientists can create new features that capture the presence or degree of outlierness. For example, a feature indicating whether a data point exceeds a certain threshold can provide the model with explicit information about extreme behavior. Alternatively, residuals from a baseline model can be used to construct features that reflect the deviation from expected values, thereby highlighting anomalies in a way that supports the modeling objective.

The treatment of outliers must also be aligned with the model being used. Some algorithms are more sensitive to outliers than others. Linear models, support vector machines, and k-nearest neighbors can be heavily influenced by extreme values, leading to unstable predictions. On the other hand, tree-based models like decision trees and random forests are generally more robust to outliers because they partition the feature space based on thresholds and are less affected by magnitude. Understanding the model's behavior helps guide the strategy for outlier handling and ensures that the chosen approach enhances rather than harms predictive performance.

Effective outlier handling in feature engineering requires a balance between preserving valuable information and protecting models from distortion. It demands a nuanced understanding of the data, the context in which it was collected, and the goals of the analysis. By thoughtfully identifying and addressing outliers, data scientists can enhance the stability, accuracy, and interpretability of their models, ultimately leading to more reliable insights and better decisions.

Encoding Categorical Variables for Modeling

Categorical variables are a common component of real-world datasets. They represent qualitative attributes that describe characteristics or labels such as gender, occupation, city, product category, or type of transaction. These variables, while informative, are not inherently suitable for use in most machine learning models, which require numerical input. As such, encoding categorical variables is an essential step in the data preprocessing and feature engineering pipeline. Choosing the right encoding technique can significantly affect model performance, complexity, and interpretability, especially when dealing with a high number of categories or interactions between features.

The fundamental challenge in encoding categorical variables lies in the fact that they do not possess any intrinsic mathematical relationship. For example, a variable representing the color of a car with values like red, blue, and green cannot be treated as ordinal or continuous. Assigning arbitrary numeric values such as 1 for red, 2 for blue, and 3 for green may imply an order that does not exist, leading to misleading interpretations by the model. Therefore, encoding must be done in a way that faithfully represents the structure of the data while making it accessible to the algorithm.

One of the most common and straightforward techniques is one-hot encoding. In this method, each unique category in a variable is transformed into a new binary column. For a variable with three categories—say, low, medium, and high—one-hot encoding would create three new columns: is_low, is_medium, and is_high. Each row in the dataset will have a 1 in the column corresponding to its category and 0s in the others. This approach works well when the number of categories is small and when there is no ordinal relationship between them. One-hot encoding preserves the categorical nature of the variable and ensures that all categories are treated equally by the model.

However, one-hot encoding has limitations, particularly when applied to high-cardinality variables, which have many unique categories. In such cases, the transformation can result in a very large number of columns, leading to a sparse and high-dimensional dataset. This not only increases computational cost but also makes the model more prone to overfitting, especially if some categories are rare and represented by very few observations. For instance, encoding a city name variable that contains thousands of unique cities can bloat the feature space and reduce model efficiency. To address this issue, other encoding techniques such as frequency encoding or target encoding are often employed.

Frequency encoding replaces each category with its frequency of occurrence in the dataset. This results in a single column where each category is represented by a numerical value corresponding to its count or proportion. The advantage of this method is that it reduces dimensionality and preserves information about the distribution of categories. However, frequency encoding may introduce unintended biases, especially if the frequency is correlated with the target variable in a way that misleads the model. For example, categories with higher frequency may be interpreted by the model as more important, even if their relationship with the target variable is weak or spurious.

Another powerful technique is target encoding, also known as mean encoding. In this approach, each category is replaced with the average value of the target variable for that category. For example, in a binary classification task, each category in the encoded variable would be assigned a value between 0 and 1, reflecting the proportion of positive outcomes associated with that category. Target encoding can capture category-level trends and improve model performance by introducing information about the target. However, it also introduces a risk of target leakage, where the model learns from information that should not be available at training time. To mitigate this risk, cross-validation techniques must be used to calculate the encoding values, ensuring that the data used to compute the mean does not include the observation being encoded.

Label encoding is another commonly used method, particularly for ordinal categorical variables. In label encoding, each category is assigned a unique integer value. This method is efficient and compact, producing a single column without increasing dimensionality. It is especially appropriate when the categories have a natural order, such as education levels or customer satisfaction ratings. However, when applied to nominal variables with no inherent order, label encoding can mislead the model into interpreting the numerical values as having mathematical significance. This can be problematic for algorithms like linear regression or support vector machines, which rely on the relationships between input values.

More sophisticated encoding methods include binary encoding, which combines the benefits of label and one-hot encoding. In binary encoding, each category is first assigned an integer value and then converted to binary form. The resulting binary digits are split into separate columns. This approach reduces the number of features compared to one-hot encoding while avoiding the implicit ordering problem of label encoding. Binary encoding is particularly effective for high-cardinality variables where one-hot encoding would be infeasible and target encoding may risk leakage.

When dealing with categorical variables, it is also important to consider the presence of unseen categories in the test set or during production deployment. Models trained on one-hot encoded data will not know how to handle new categories that were not present in the training set. This can lead to missing values or errors during inference. One way to address this is by including a generic unknown category during training or by using encoding techniques that can gracefully handle new categories, such as hashing. Hashing trick encodes categories into a fixed number of columns using a hash function, allowing for a compact representation that can accommodate previously unseen values. However, it introduces a risk of collisions, where different categories are mapped to the same hash bucket, potentially reducing model performance.

Another consideration is the interpretability of the encoded features. Some encoding methods, such as one-hot and label encoding, are easy to reverse and understand, making them suitable for models that require transparency and explainability. Others, like target or hashing encoding, may create features that are difficult to interpret, which can be a drawback in applications where understanding the model's behavior is crucial. The choice of encoding method must therefore align with the overall goals of the project, whether they prioritize accuracy, efficiency, or interpretability.

Encoding categorical variables is not a trivial preprocessing step but a critical part of feature engineering that can shape the outcome of a machine learning pipeline. The choice of encoding technique depends on the data's characteristics, the number and type of categories, the model to be used, and the importance of interpretability. An effective encoding strategy transforms qualitative information into a form that models can understand and learn from, ultimately bridging the gap between raw categorical data and predictive insights.

Numerical Feature Transformation Techniques

Numerical features are the backbone of most machine learning models. They capture measurable quantities such as age, income, temperature, distance, and time. However, raw numerical data is not always in a form that can be directly used by modeling algorithms. The presence of skewed distributions, varying scales, outliers, and non-linear relationships can hinder the model's ability to learn meaningful patterns. To address these challenges, numerical feature transformation techniques are applied during the feature engineering process. These transformations adjust the structure or scale of numerical variables in ways that enhance model performance, improve convergence, and in some cases, reveal hidden relationships within the data.

One of the primary reasons for transforming numerical features is to handle skewed data distributions. Many real-world numerical variables are not normally distributed. For example, income is often heavily right-skewed, meaning a small number of individuals have extremely high earnings compared to the majority. Machine learning models, particularly linear models and algorithms that assume Gaussian distributions, may perform poorly on such skewed data. Applying transformations such as the logarithmic, square root, or cube root can help to reduce skewness, making the distribution more symmetric and easier for the model to interpret. Log transformation is particularly effective when dealing with data that spans several orders of magnitude, as it compresses the scale and brings extreme values closer to the center.

Normalization is another key technique for transforming numerical features. It involves scaling data to a specific range, typically between 0 and 1. This is important for algorithms that rely on distance metrics, such as k-nearest neighbors or support vector machines, where features with larger numerical ranges can dominate the calculation of distances and distort the results. Normalization ensures that each feature contributes equally to the model. Min-max scaling is a common normalization method, where each value is adjusted based on the minimum and maximum of the feature. While simple, this method is sensitive to outliers, which can compress the majority of the data into a narrow band.

Standardization is an alternative scaling technique that transforms data to have a mean of zero and a standard deviation of one. This is particularly useful for algorithms like logistic regression, principal component analysis, and gradient descent-based models, which are sensitive to the scale of the input variables. Standardization does not bound the values between fixed limits, allowing for a wider spread of transformed values. It is more robust than min-max normalization when the data contains outliers, as it centers the data based on statistical moments rather than absolute range.

In addition to scaling and normalization, polynomial transformation is a method used to capture non-linear relationships between features and the target variable. By introducing polynomial terms, such as the square or cube of an original feature, the model gains the ability to represent more complex patterns in the data. This is especially helpful for linear models, which are otherwise limited to linear relationships. For instance, the effect of age on a target outcome might not be linear; people in middle age might show different behavior compared to the very young or the elderly. Polynomial transformation allows the model to better capture such trends by adding curvature to the prediction space.

Interaction terms represent another important transformation technique. These are created by multiplying two or more features together to capture the combined effect of variables that may influence the target in a non-additive way. For example, the product of education level and years of experience might be more predictive of salary than either feature alone. Interaction terms can reveal dependencies and joint influences that would otherwise be missed in a simple additive model. Care must be taken, however, to avoid an explosion in dimensionality when creating multiple interaction terms, as this can increase the risk of overfitting and reduce model interpretability.

Discretization, or binning, is a transformation that converts continuous numerical features into categorical ones by dividing the range into intervals. This can simplify the modeling process and make it easier to capture non-linear patterns. For example, a continuous variable like age can be divided into age groups such as 0–18, 19–35, 36–60, and 60+. This approach can help reduce the impact of noise and minor fluctuations in the data, especially in decision tree-based models that often perform better with categorical splits. Binning can be done based on equal width, equal frequency, or custom domain-specific thresholds. However, discretization reduces the granularity of the data and may lead to a loss of information if not done carefully.

Clipping is another transformation technique used to handle extreme values without removing them. This involves setting a lower and upper bound for a feature, and any values outside this range are clipped to the boundary values. Clipping helps control the influence of outliers without eliminating potentially useful data points. It is especially useful when a small number of extreme values are distorting the overall distribution, affecting scaling, or introducing instability in the model.

Rank transformation is useful in scenarios where the distribution of a variable does not matter, but its relative ordering does. In this method, each value is replaced by its rank in the sorted list of values. Rank-based transformations are non-parametric and robust to outliers. They are often used in statistical modeling when the data violates normality assumptions, or in ensemble methods that combine predictions based on ordering rather than magnitude.

Quantile transformation is another advanced technique that maps the original values to a uniform or normal distribution based on their quantiles. This method is powerful when a model performs better with input features that resemble a specific distribution. It is often used in preprocessing pipelines where model sensitivity to distributional properties needs to be minimized. By forcing the data into a uniform or Gaussian shape, quantile transformation helps standardize feature behavior across different inputs.

Box-Cox and Yeo-Johnson transformations are flexible techniques for stabilizing variance and making data more normal-like. They are particularly helpful when preparing data for algorithms that assume linear relationships and normal distributions. The Box-Cox transformation requires strictly positive input values, whereas Yeo-

Johnson can handle both positive and negative values. These transformations estimate an optimal parameter for reshaping the data, automatically adapting to the distribution's characteristics.

Transforming numerical features is both a technical and strategic task. Each technique brings with it a set of assumptions, advantages, and trade-offs that must be carefully weighed. The effectiveness of a transformation depends not only on the mathematical correctness but also on the context of the data and the goals of the analysis. By thoughtfully applying numerical transformations, data scientists can improve model accuracy, accelerate training convergence, and reveal hidden relationships, all of which are vital for developing robust and interpretable machine learning solutions.

Binning and Discretization Strategies

Binning and discretization are powerful techniques in feature engineering used to convert continuous numerical variables into categorical counterparts. These strategies can enhance the performance and interpretability of models, particularly those that work well with categorical data or where non-linear relationships are more easily captured through grouped intervals. Discretizing numerical features can also help mitigate the influence of noise or outliers, simplify the structure of the data, and highlight meaningful thresholds or trends that might otherwise be obscured in raw continuous values. However, applying binning effectively requires a solid understanding of both the data and the modeling context, as poorly executed binning can degrade performance or introduce unintended bias.

The most basic form of binning is equal-width binning, where the range of a variable is divided into intervals of equal size. For example, a variable representing age from 0 to 100 might be split into five bins of width 20: 0–20, 21–40, 41–60, 61–80, and 81–100. Each data point is then assigned to a bin based on its value. This method is simple to implement and interpret, making it popular for exploratory analysis and early-stage modeling. However, equal-width binning assumes that the distribution of values is uniform, which is rarely the case in real-world datasets. If the data is skewed or contains clusters, equal-width bins may result in imbalanced groupings, where some bins have very few observations and others are overloaded. This imbalance can negatively affect the model's ability to learn patterns effectively.

To address this issue, equal-frequency binning, also known as quantile binning, divides the data into bins such that each bin contains approximately the same number of observations. For example, if a dataset contains 1000 observations, equal-frequency binning into five bins would ensure each bin contains around 200 observations, regardless of the range of values. This technique is more robust to skewed distributions and can be particularly effective when the goal is to balance class representation across bins. However, it can produce bins with highly variable widths, making interpretation less straightforward. Two bins might have vastly different ranges, yet contain the same number of observations. This can be problematic if the real-world meaning of the variable is tied to the magnitude of its values, rather than just their distribution.

Another useful approach is custom binning, where domain knowledge or data-driven insights guide the creation of bins with specific boundaries. In some industries, natural thresholds exist that define meaningful categories. For instance, in finance, credit scores might be grouped into poor, fair, good, and excellent based on standardized cutoffs used by lenders. Similarly, in healthcare, age ranges might be aligned with risk categories, such as pediatric, adult, and elderly. Custom binning enables the incorporation of expert knowledge into the feature set, allowing models to leverage relevant distinctions that are not apparent from distributional analysis alone. This strategy enhances interpretability and often aligns better with decision-making processes in business or clinical settings.

Decision tree algorithms offer a data-driven way to determine optimal binning thresholds. By analyzing how the target variable changes across the range of a feature, decision trees identify splits that maximize information gain or reduce impurity. The resulting splits can be used as bin edges, converting the continuous variable into a categorical one that captures the most predictive value. This technique, known as supervised discretization, tailors the binning process to the outcome of interest, improving the alignment between features and the target. However, it risks overfitting if the splits are too specific to the training data, especially in small datasets or when the relationship between the feature and target is unstable.

Clustering algorithms can also be employed for binning, particularly when the data shows complex patterns not captured by simple thresholds. K-means clustering, for example, can be applied to a single numerical feature to group similar values into clusters. Each cluster then forms a bin, with all values assigned to the same group labeled with a common identifier. This unsupervised approach does not consider the target variable but can uncover natural groupings that reflect underlying structure in the data. It is especially useful when the feature has multimodal distributions or when there is no obvious domain-based logic for choosing bin boundaries.

While binning simplifies continuous variables, it also introduces certain limitations. One major drawback is the potential loss of information. By grouping a range of values into a single category, binning can obscure subtle variations and reduce the granularity of the data. For example, a person aged 31 and another aged 39 might both fall into the same age bin of 30–40, even though they may exhibit different behaviors or risk profiles. If these differences are relevant to the prediction task, the model may suffer from decreased accuracy. Therefore, binning should be used judiciously, especially when the model benefits from nuanced patterns in the original continuous variable.

Another challenge is ensuring consistency between training and testing data. Once binning rules are established on the training set, they must be applied identically to all future data, including validation and production data. Any discrepancies in binning logic or boundaries can result in errors or degraded performance. This requires careful implementation of binning pipelines, where transformation steps are saved and reapplied consistently. In modern machine learning workflows, this is typically handled through tools such as scikit-learn's pipelines or custom feature transformation modules that ensure reproducibility and robustness.

Feature scaling is another consideration in the context of binning. Since binned variables are no longer continuous, they are typically not subjected to standard scaling or normalization. Instead, they are treated as categorical features, often requiring encoding methods such as one-hot or ordinal encoding before being fed into a model. This shift changes the way models interpret the variable and affects how they interact with other features. Understanding this transformation is key to maintaining the integrity and interpretability of the model.

In some scenarios, binning can also improve model robustness and generalization. By reducing the complexity of the feature space and limiting the impact of noise or outliers, discretized variables can help models focus on broader trends rather than overfitting to fine-grained fluctuations. This is particularly beneficial in noisy or unstable datasets, where precision in the raw values is not as important as the general magnitude or category. It can also simplify communication of results to stakeholders, as grouped features are often more intuitive and easier to understand than continuous metrics.

Ultimately, binning and discretization are not merely technical procedures, but strategic decisions that shape the way models perceive and learn from data. When executed thoughtfully, these transformations can enhance both performance and interpretability, bridge the gap between data science and domain knowledge, and contribute to more robust and transparent predictive systems.

Scaling and Normalization for Consistent Features

In the domain of feature engineering, scaling and normalization are foundational techniques used to prepare numerical data for modeling. These transformations ensure that numerical features contribute appropriately to the learning process, especially when their ranges differ significantly. Without proper scaling or normalization, models can behave unpredictably, place undue weight on certain features, or fail to converge efficiently. Scaling and normalization do not change the underlying relationships in the data but instead reformat the input so that machine learning algorithms can interpret and process it more effectively.

When working with real-world datasets, it is common to encounter numerical features with varying scales. One feature might represent temperature in degrees Celsius ranging from -10 to 40, while another could be income values ranging from a few hundred to several hundred thousand. In such scenarios, features with larger numeric ranges can dominate the training process, particularly in algorithms that are sensitive to the magnitude of input values. Models that rely on distance calculations, such as k-nearest neighbors or support vector machines, are especially vulnerable to inconsistencies in feature scale. The distance between two data points in a high-dimensional space is influenced heavily by the largest-scale variables, skewing the results and diminishing the contribution of smaller-scale features.

Scaling addresses this issue by adjusting the feature values so that they fall within a more uniform range. One of the most widely used scaling techniques is min-max scaling, which transforms each feature to a specified range, typically between zero and one. This transformation is achieved by subtracting the minimum value of the feature and dividing by the range. While min-max scaling is straightforward and effective for many applications, it is sensitive to outliers. Extreme values can stretch the range and compress the majority of the data into a narrow band, reducing the expressiveness of the transformation.

Standardization, on the other hand, transforms features to have a mean of zero and a standard deviation of one. This is achieved by subtracting the mean and dividing by the standard deviation. Standardization is particularly useful when features are normally distributed or when the goal is to center the data around zero. This technique is more robust to outliers compared to min-max scaling, as it does not depend on the absolute minimum or maximum values of the feature. Standardization is also preferred in algorithms that assume a Gaussian distribution of inputs, such as logistic regression or linear discriminant analysis.

In many modeling scenarios, especially those involving gradient descent, scaling can accelerate convergence by ensuring that each feature has a similar impact on the cost function. When features are on drastically different scales, the gradient steps taken during optimization may be skewed toward the dimensions with larger values, making the optimization path inefficient or unstable. Properly scaled features help maintain a balanced learning rate across dimensions, resulting in faster and more stable model training. In neural networks, feature scaling is essential to prevent activation functions from saturating. If input values are too large or too small, functions like the sigmoid or tanh can become saturated, resulting in vanishing gradients and poor learning.

Normalization, distinct from standardization, typically refers to the process of adjusting individual samples so that their vector norm equals one. This technique is useful in text classification, image processing, or recommendation systems where the relative importance of features within a single sample matters more than the absolute value across samples. Normalization is commonly applied when working with sparse data, such as TF-IDF matrices in natural language processing, where each document vector is scaled to have unit length. This ensures that comparisons between documents are based on their relative patterns rather than magnitude, facilitating more accurate similarity measures.

Another important consideration is the presence of categorical variables that have been numerically encoded. Features such as zip codes or product IDs may be represented as integers, but they do not have a true numerical relationship. Scaling these features can introduce unintended assumptions about their magnitude or order, misleading the model. Therefore, not all numeric-looking features should be scaled or normalized, especially when they are inherently categorical in nature.

Robust scaling methods have been developed to address the challenges posed by outliers. One such method uses the median and interquartile range instead of the mean and standard deviation. Robust scalers transform data by subtracting the median and dividing by the interquartile range, which makes them less sensitive to extreme values. This approach is particularly beneficial when the dataset contains anomalies or outliers that are valid and should be preserved but not allowed to distort the overall transformation. By focusing on the central tendency and spread of the middle portion of the data, robust scaling provides a more resilient transformation suitable for skewed or heavy-tailed distributions.

Feature scaling and normalization are not only essential during the training phase but must also be consistently applied to any new data used for prediction. Once a transformation is learned from the training data, the same transformation parameters must be applied to the test set or to production inputs. Failure to do so leads to inconsistencies that can degrade model performance. In modern data science workflows, this is addressed by including scaling transformations as part of a preprocessing pipeline that ensures reproducibility and consistency across all stages of model deployment.

It is also important to consider the interpretability of scaled features. In some applications, such as healthcare or finance, stakeholders may require explanations for model decisions based on original feature values. When features are scaled, the direct relationship between the transformed values and real-world quantities becomes obscured. This can be addressed by retaining a mapping between original and transformed values or by post-processing model outputs to provide explanations in the original feature space. Interpretability should be weighed against performance gains when deciding whether and how to apply scaling.

The effectiveness of scaling and normalization also depends on the type of model being used. Tree-based models, such as decision trees, random forests, and gradient boosting machines, are inherently insensitive to feature scale. These models split data based on threshold values, and their performance is not influenced by the magnitude of the feature values. For such models, scaling may be unnecessary and can be skipped altogether. However, for models based on linear relationships, distance measures, or gradient optimization, proper scaling is a critical step that ensures consistent and reliable learning behavior.

In the broader context of feature engineering, scaling and normalization are part of a toolkit that transforms raw data into forms that are compatible with algorithmic assumptions and computational processes. They are often applied in conjunction with other transformations, such as outlier handling, binning, or encoding, forming a comprehensive preprocessing pipeline. Understanding when and how to apply these techniques allows data scientists to build models that are both performant and robust, regardless of the diversity and complexity of the input features.

Text Feature Engineering Using NLP Techniques

Text data is one of the most abundant and valuable forms of unstructured data available in the digital world. From social media posts and customer reviews to legal documents and medical records, textual information is pervasive across industries. However, raw text is not directly usable by most machine learning algorithms, which require structured numerical input. Transforming text into meaningful numerical features is the core objective of text feature engineering, and it plays a vital role in natural language processing tasks. Leveraging effective NLP techniques allows data scientists to extract semantic, syntactic, and contextual information from language, enabling models to perform sentiment analysis, classification, recommendation, and more with greater accuracy and insight.

The initial step in text feature engineering is text preprocessing. Raw text often contains noise, inconsistencies, and irrelevant symbols such as punctuation, HTML tags, or special characters. These elements must be cleaned to ensure that the downstream features capture the linguistic content rather than formatting artifacts. Tokenization is a foundational operation that breaks down text into individual units, typically words or subwords. It allows for the creation of features at a granular level and serves as the basis for most NLP pipelines. After tokenization, text is commonly transformed to lowercase to standardize the tokens, reducing redundancy due to capitalization differences.

Stopword removal is another common preprocessing step. Stopwords are frequently occurring words such as "the," "and," or "in" that usually carry little discriminative value in many NLP tasks. By removing them, the focus shifts to the more informative content words. However, the decision to exclude stopwords depends on the specific application. In some cases, function words can be important, such as when analyzing writing style, detecting sarcasm, or capturing negation. Lemmatization and stemming further reduce tokens to their root or base form. These processes consolidate similar words into a single feature, decreasing vocabulary size and improving generalization. Lemmatization uses linguistic rules to convert words into their base form, while stemming applies a more aggressive, rule-based truncation that may not always yield valid words.

Once the text has been preprocessed, the next task is to convert it into numerical form. One of the earliest and most intuitive approaches is the bag-of-words model. This method represents text as a vector of word counts, disregarding grammar and word order but preserving frequency information. While simple, it captures basic lexical content and can be effective for tasks like document classification or spam detection. The bag-of-words model can be further refined with term frequency-inverse document frequency (TF-IDF), which adjusts word counts based on their importance. Words that appear frequently across many documents are given lower weights, while rare but potentially informative words are emphasized. This weighting scheme helps distinguish common words from those that are more uniquely associated with specific topics or categories.

Despite their utility, both bag-of-words and TF-IDF result in high-dimensional, sparse vectors that ignore word order and semantic relationships. To address this limitation, word embeddings were introduced. Word embeddings represent words as dense vectors in a continuous space, capturing semantic similarity through geometric proximity. Techniques like Word2Vec and GloVe learn embeddings based on word co-occurrence patterns in large corpora. These models place similar words close together in the embedding space, allowing models to recognize relationships such as synonyms, analogies, or thematic associations. Embeddings can be averaged across a sentence or document to produce fixed-length feature vectors for modeling. Although simple, this method captures more semantic richness than count-based approaches.

More advanced embedding techniques include context-aware models like ELMo, BERT, and RoBERTa. These models generate word representations that depend on the surrounding context, allowing them to differentiate between polysemous words—those with multiple meanings depending on usage. For instance, the word "bank" would be represented differently in the context of a river versus a financial institution. These models rely on deep neural networks and transformer architectures that have been pre-trained on massive datasets. Fine-tuning these models for specific tasks can yield state-of-the-art performance in many NLP applications. Extracting features from intermediate layers of such models provides a powerful way to integrate deep contextual understanding into downstream machine learning workflows.

Beyond word-level features, higher-order linguistic features can also enhance text representations. Part-of-speech tagging identifies the grammatical role of each word, such as noun, verb, or adjective. These tags can be used as features to capture syntactic patterns that are relevant to the task. Named entity recognition identifies specific entities like people, organizations, locations, or dates. These entities can be used to create features indicating the presence of certain types of information or to extract structured data from unstructured text. Dependency parsing reveals the grammatical structure of a sentence by identifying relationships between words, such as subject-verb-object structures. These relationships can be useful for understanding sentence meaning and creating features that reflect logical or causal connections.

Another dimension of text feature engineering involves the use of n-grams. An n-gram is a sequence of n consecutive words or characters in the text. Unigrams represent single words, bigrams capture two-word sequences, and so on. Including n-grams allows models to capture short phrases or collocations that convey specific meaning. For example, the bigram "not good" has a different sentiment than the sum of its parts. However, using n-grams can significantly increase the dimensionality of the feature space, so careful tuning and feature selection are necessary to avoid overfitting and maintain computational efficiency.

In some cases, sentiment or emotion features are explicitly engineered using external lexicons or pretrained models. These features quantify the emotional tone of a document or sentence and are particularly useful in applications like product review analysis, public opinion mining, or customer service automation. Polarity scores, subjectivity measures, or emotion tags can be derived and included as features alongside traditional text representations.

The final aspect of text feature engineering lies in combining and enriching features. Text data often contains metadata such as author, timestamp, or source, which can be integrated into the feature set. Combining text-derived features with structured data features provides a more comprehensive view of each instance, enabling models to capture patterns that span both language and context. Additionally, dimensionality reduction techniques such as principal component analysis or truncated singular value decomposition can be applied to large text feature sets to reduce noise and improve generalization.

Text feature engineering using NLP techniques is a dynamic and evolving field. It requires a blend of linguistic insight, statistical intuition, and computational skill to transform unstructured text into structured, meaningful representations that drive predictive performance. By carefully selecting and engineering features that reflect both the surface and deep structures of language, data scientists can unlock the vast potential of text data and empower models to interpret and act upon human communication in all its complexity.

Vectorizing Text with Count and TF-IDF

Converting raw text into a format that can be processed by machine learning algorithms is a fundamental challenge in natural language processing. Unlike numerical data, text is unstructured and composed of sequences of words that carry meaning based on context, grammar, and semantics. For machines to understand and analyze text, it must be transformed into numerical vectors that represent the underlying information in a structured format. Two foundational methods for achieving this transformation are count vectorization and term frequency-inverse document frequency, commonly known as TF-IDF. These approaches form the basis of many traditional NLP pipelines and continue to be widely used for tasks such as document classification, sentiment analysis, spam detection, and topic modeling.

Count vectorization is the most straightforward technique for converting text into numerical form. In this method, a vocabulary is first built from the entire corpus of documents. Each unique word becomes a feature in the vector representation, and each document is represented as a vector indicating the number of times each word from the vocabulary appears in it. This approach is also known as the bag-of-words model, where the order of words is disregarded, and only the presence or frequency of words is captured. Despite its simplicity, the bag-of-words model is effective in capturing lexical content and has been successfully applied in many classification and retrieval tasks.

One of the strengths of count vectorization is its transparency and ease of interpretation. Each dimension of the resulting vector corresponds to a specific word, and the value indicates the frequency of that word in the document. This direct mapping makes it easy to analyze and understand the influence of individual words on model predictions. However, count vectors suffer from several limitations. First, they result in high-dimensional and sparse representations, especially when the vocabulary is large. Most documents use only a small subset of the entire vocabulary, leading to vectors filled with zeros. This sparsity can pose computational challenges and may affect the performance of some algorithms that are sensitive to the curse of dimensionality.

Another issue with count vectorization is that it treats all words equally, regardless of their importance or informativeness. Common words like "the," "is," or "and" may appear frequently across all documents, contributing to high counts but offering little value in distinguishing between texts. In contrast, rare words that are highly specific to certain documents may carry more discriminative power. To address this imbalance, the TF-IDF method was introduced. TF-IDF improves upon count vectorization by weighting each word's frequency in a document by how rare it is across the entire corpus. This weighting scheme highlights terms that are particularly informative for individual documents while downplaying those that are common across the dataset.

The TF-IDF value for a word is calculated by multiplying its term frequency (TF) by its inverse document frequency (IDF). Term frequency measures how often a word appears in a document, often normalized by the total number of words in that document. This normalization accounts for document length and ensures that longer documents do not unfairly dominate the counts. Inverse document frequency, on the other hand, measures how unique a word is across all documents. It is computed as the logarithm of the ratio of the total number of documents to the number of documents that contain the word, typically with smoothing to prevent division by zero. As a result, words that appear in many documents receive lower weights, while words that are rare but concentrated in a few documents receive higher scores.

TF-IDF vectors tend to be more balanced and informative than raw count vectors. They help models focus on the unique content of each document rather than the general structure of the language. For example, in a collection of news articles, common words like "government" or "economy" might appear frequently across topics, but words like "inflation" or "immigration" might be specific to certain themes. TF-IDF helps differentiate articles by emphasizing these topic-specific terms. Moreover, TF-IDF vectors are often better suited for similarity-based tasks, such as document clustering or search engines, where measuring the relative importance of words is crucial for comparing texts.

Despite its advantages, TF-IDF is not without limitations. Like count vectorization, it still produces sparse and high-dimensional vectors. It also does not account for the semantics or order of words. Words with similar meanings but different spellings or synonyms are treated as distinct features, and contextual information is lost. Additionally, TF-IDF assumes a linear relationship between word frequency and importance, which may not always reflect how humans interpret language. Nevertheless, TF-IDF remains a valuable tool due to its simplicity, scalability, and interpretability.

Practical implementations of count and TF-IDF vectorization are widely available in machine learning libraries such as scikit-learn. These implementations allow for additional customization, such as limiting the size of the vocabulary, setting a minimum or maximum document frequency threshold, and choosing between different normalization methods. Such controls help tailor the vectorization process to the characteristics of the dataset and the goals of the task.

For example, excluding very rare or very common words can reduce noise and improve model generalization.

Another extension of these techniques involves the use of n-grams instead of single words. An n-gram is a sequence of n consecutive tokens, and incorporating n-grams into count or TF-IDF vectorization allows the model to capture short phrases and word combinations that carry specific meaning. For instance, the bigram "not good" conveys negative sentiment, which would be lost if only unigrams were considered. Including n-grams enhances the expressive power of the vector representation, although it also increases dimensionality, requiring careful tuning to avoid overfitting and performance degradation.

In many modern NLP workflows, count and TF-IDF vectorization still play a crucial role, especially when paired with traditional machine learning models like logistic regression, support vector machines, or naïve Bayes classifiers. These models can perform remarkably well on tasks like spam detection, topic categorization, and sentiment analysis when combined with well-engineered text features. While deep learning and contextual embeddings have expanded the frontiers of text representation, the interpretability, efficiency, and ease of use of count and TF-IDF vectorization ensure their continued relevance in practical applications.

Vectorizing text with count and TF-IDF methods transforms language into a structured numerical form that machines can understand. These techniques bridge the gap between unstructured text and statistical models, providing a foundation for many natural language processing tasks. By capturing both frequency and informativeness of words, they enable models to learn from textual patterns and make accurate predictions. The success of these methods lies in their balance between simplicity and effectiveness, making them indispensable tools in the feature engineering toolkit for text-based machine learning.

Feature Engineering for Time Series Data

Time series data presents a unique set of challenges and opportunities in feature engineering due to its sequential and temporal nature. Unlike standard tabular data where observations are assumed to be independent and identically distributed, time series data consists of ordered observations where past values often influence future outcomes. This temporal dependency must be respected and leveraged when creating features, as ignoring it can result in poorly performing models and invalid conclusions. Feature engineering for time series involves extracting meaningful information from time-based sequences that helps machine learning models capture trends, seasonality, patterns, and temporal dependencies inherent in the data.

The foundation of any time series feature engineering process begins with the decomposition of time itself. The timestamp associated with each observation can be used to derive a rich set of temporal features. These include the day of the week, day of the month, month, quarter, year, hour, and even minute, depending on the granularity of the data. Such features help capture recurring patterns, such as increased sales on weekends, higher web traffic during specific hours, or seasonal trends across months or quarters. These extracted time components can be encoded and used as categorical or numerical variables to inform the model of cyclical behaviors in the data.

A key concept in time series feature engineering is the use of lag features. These are features that incorporate the value of a variable from previous time steps. For example, in forecasting electricity consumption, the current consumption may depend heavily on the value from the previous hour, day, or week. By creating lag features for one or more previous time steps, the model is given access to past values that it can use to understand temporal dynamics. The selection of appropriate lag intervals is critical and often informed by domain knowledge or autocorrelation analysis, which helps identify the strength of relationships between different time lags.

Another valuable set of features in time series analysis comes from rolling or moving window statistics. These involve calculating summary statistics such as mean, median, standard deviation, minimum, or maximum over a fixed window of previous time points.

Rolling features help smooth out short-term fluctuations and reveal local trends or variability in the data. For example, a rolling mean of stock prices over the last ten days can serve as a momentum indicator, while rolling standard deviation may indicate volatility. The window size must be chosen carefully, balancing the need to capture meaningful variation without over-smoothing or introducing excessive lag.

Differencing is a technique that transforms a time series by subtracting the value at the previous time step from the current value. This is especially useful for making non-stationary data more stationary, which is a common requirement for many time series models. First-order differencing removes linear trends, while higher-order differencing can be applied for more complex structures. While differencing is often associated with traditional statistical models like ARIMA, it also serves as a powerful transformation for creating features that emphasize changes over time, rather than absolute values.

Cyclical encoding is another important transformation for time series data, especially when working with features like hours of the day, days of the week, or months of the year. These time components are inherently cyclical in nature, meaning that after reaching a maximum value, they wrap around to the beginning again. Simply treating them as integers introduces artificial discontinuities into the data. To preserve the cyclical structure, sine and cosine transformations can be used. For example, the hour of the day can be represented by two features: sine of the hour scaled to a 24-hour cycle, and cosine of the same. This allows models to recognize that hour 23 and hour 0 are actually adjacent in time, rather than distant, as they would appear with linear encoding.

External or exogenous features are often included in time series feature engineering to enhance predictive power. These might include calendar events, weather data, holidays, promotional campaigns, or economic indicators that influence the target variable. For instance, a spike in retail sales during a holiday season can be captured by incorporating a binary feature indicating the presence of a holiday. Weather variables such as temperature or precipitation can be crucial in energy demand forecasting or agriculture yield prediction. By aligning these external datasets with the primary time series and engineering relevant features, models can account for factors beyond the internal history of the series.

One of the more advanced approaches to time series feature engineering involves extracting frequency domain characteristics. This includes techniques such as Fourier transforms or wavelet decompositions that analyze the data in terms of frequency components. These transformations can uncover hidden periodicities or cyclic behaviors that are not easily detectable in the time domain. Features derived from frequency analysis are particularly useful in domains such as signal processing, audio analysis, and financial modeling, where data often contains multiple overlapping patterns operating at different frequencies.

The handling of missing data in time series also demands special attention. Unlike static datasets, where missing values can be imputed based on overall statistics, time series data often requires forward or backward filling to preserve the sequence. Interpolation techniques that maintain the temporal structure are crucial to avoid introducing bias or breaks in the data. In some cases, the pattern of missingness itself can be informative and engineered as a separate feature, especially if data collection is influenced by external conditions.

Seasonal decomposition is another technique that can be used to extract structured components from a time series. By separating the trend, seasonal, and residual components, features can be engineered that represent each of these aspects independently. These components can then be fed into models to improve interpretability and performance. For example, the trend component can highlight long-term movement, while the seasonal component can show regular fluctuations associated with specific time periods.

Ultimately, time series feature engineering is not just about transforming data; it is about encoding temporal knowledge and patterns into a format that models can understand. This process requires a deep understanding of the domain, the nature of the time series, and the modeling objectives. Whether using simple lag features or complex frequency transformations, the goal remains the same: to extract relevant signals from the noise of temporal data. By creating features that respect and leverage the temporal structure, data scientists can build models that not only predict future outcomes accurately but also uncover insights into the dynamics of time-dependent phenomena.

Lag Features and Rolling Statistics

Lag features and rolling statistics are among the most fundamental and powerful tools in time series feature engineering. These techniques are designed to capture temporal dependencies and local patterns that occur over time, allowing models to learn from past behavior in order to make accurate predictions about the future. In time series data, each observation is inherently linked to a point in time, and the relationship between past and present values often holds critical information. Whether forecasting stock prices, predicting energy consumption, or modeling traffic flow, incorporating historical patterns through lag and rolling features significantly enhances model performance and interpretability.

Lag features are created by shifting a time series variable by one or more time steps to use its past values as predictors. For example, if the current value of interest is at time t, lag features might include the value at t–1, t–2, t–3, and so on. These lags allow the model to understand how the current state depends on past behavior. In many real-world applications, the most recent past values carry the strongest signal for predicting the near future. For instance, in electricity demand forecasting, the load observed in the previous hour or the same hour the day before often plays a significant role in estimating the current hour's demand. The number and spacing of lags selected depend on the domain knowledge, autocorrelation analysis, and specific business needs.

Autocorrelation and partial autocorrelation plots are useful diagnostic tools for identifying meaningful lags. These plots show the correlation of a time series with its past values at various lags, helping data scientists determine which lags contain predictive information. Selecting too few lags might miss important patterns, while including too many can lead to overfitting and increased model complexity. Additionally, domain expertise can guide the selection of lags that reflect known periodicities, such as daily, weekly, or seasonal cycles. In retail data, for instance, sales patterns often repeat every seven days, suggesting the inclusion of a lag that represents the same day of the previous week.

While lag features capture specific points in the past, rolling statistics summarize the behavior of a variable over a moving window of time. A rolling window calculates a statistic such as the mean, median, minimum, maximum, or standard deviation over a fixed number of previous observations. This approach smooths out short-term fluctuations and captures trends, volatility, or changes in distribution over time. Rolling features are especially helpful in understanding the context in which a current observation occurs. For example, the average temperature over the past seven days can provide more insight into a weather pattern than a single day's reading. Similarly, rolling volatility in financial markets can be more indicative of risk than point-in-time price changes.

The size of the rolling window is a critical hyperparameter in creating rolling statistics. A small window captures very short-term trends but may be overly sensitive to noise, while a large window provides more stability at the cost of responsiveness. The choice of window size should reflect the underlying frequency and periodicity of the data. In financial time series, a 20-day rolling mean might be used to represent a monthly trend, while in hourly sensor data, a 24-hour window might be more appropriate to detect daily cycles. Moreover, multiple rolling statistics with different window sizes can be created in parallel to give the model access to short, medium, and long-term perspectives.

Expanding windows, or cumulative statistics, are a variant of rolling statistics where the window grows with time, including all past observations up to the current point. This technique is useful when it is important to account for the full historical context rather than a fixed window. For example, cumulative sums or means provide insights into long-term trends or total accumulation, such as total revenue to date or the average error rate over time. Unlike rolling windows, expanding features tend to smooth out temporary fluctuations and emphasize structural shifts in the data.

Lag and rolling features can also be engineered from external or exogenous variables, not just the primary target variable. For example, in forecasting sales, lag features might be derived from promotional activity, advertising spend, or website traffic, which may have delayed effects on outcomes. Including lags of such variables enables the model to capture the influence of past external factors on present behavior. Similarly, rolling statistics of these variables, such as average ad spend over the past week, provide temporal summaries that add richness to the model's understanding of context.

A crucial consideration when engineering lag and rolling features is data leakage. Since time series models must predict future values without access to future data, care must be taken to ensure that lag and rolling computations are based only on past observations. This is especially important when splitting data into training and test sets or performing cross-validation. Features must be created using only information available up to the prediction point, otherwise the model may learn from information it would not have in a real-world deployment, resulting in misleadingly optimistic performance.

Lag and rolling features are not only applicable to the target variable but can also be constructed for any relevant predictor. In multivariate time series, relationships between different variables may exhibit temporal lag. For instance, in industrial settings, sensor readings from one component might influence another with a delay. Capturing these relationships through lag features allows the model to learn interdependencies and cause-effect sequences that improve forecasting accuracy and system understanding.

In many applications, transformations of lag and rolling features also prove valuable. Differencing lag values can reveal momentum or acceleration, such as the rate of change from one time step to another. Combining lag values to create ratios, such as the current value divided by the rolling mean, allows for the detection of anomalies or deviations from expected behavior. These engineered features help the model detect unusual events, sudden spikes, or structural breaks in the time series that would otherwise be hidden in raw values.

Visualization is often an essential step in developing and validating lag and rolling features. Plotting the original series alongside its lagged versions and rolling statistics can reveal how well these engineered features capture trends and patterns. Visual inspection can also help diagnose problems such as window misalignment or unintended smoothing. Incorporating visual feedback into the feature engineering process ensures that the features make intuitive and statistical sense before being passed into models.

Ultimately, lag features and rolling statistics translate the temporal structure of time series data into quantifiable patterns that machine learning models can recognize and learn from. These features capture both point-in-time influences and contextual trends, providing a bridge between raw sequences and predictive insight. When thoughtfully constructed and rigorously validated, lag and rolling features become essential components of any effective time series modeling strategy.

Cyclical Encoding of Time-based Variables

Time-based variables are central to many machine learning problems, especially in domains such as retail, finance, energy, transportation, and web analytics. Features like hour of the day, day of the week, month of the year, and day of the year often capture essential periodic patterns that affect the target variable. However, these features possess a unique characteristic: they are cyclical in nature. Unlike linear variables, where the distance between two values is constant and meaningful in both directions, cyclical variables wrap around after a certain point. For instance, the hour after 23:00 is 00:00, not 24:00, and December is immediately followed by January. This cyclicality must be respected when encoding time-based variables for use in machine learning models. Failing to do so can lead to distorted representations and hinder a model's ability to learn from temporal patterns.

The core issue with naive encoding of cyclical variables lies in the misleading interpretation of numerical proximity. If we represent hours as integers from 0 to 23, a model may interpret 23 and 0 as being far apart, while in reality, they are adjacent in the cycle of a day. The same applies to days of the week, where Sunday (6) and Monday (0) are next to each other, but numerically they appear distant. Linear encoding, where values are simply represented by integers, introduces artificial discontinuities that break the natural flow of the cycle. This misrepresentation can result in poor model performance, particularly when using algorithms sensitive to numeric distance, such as linear regression, k-nearest neighbors, or neural networks.

To address this challenge, cyclical encoding techniques transform time-based variables into a format that preserves their circular structure. The most widely used method involves representing each cyclical variable using a pair of sine and cosine transformations. This approach maps the variable onto a unit circle, ensuring that the endpoints of the cycle are adjacent in the transformed space. For example, to encode the hour of the day, we can apply the transformation $\sin(2\pi * \text{hour} / 24)$ and $\cos(2\pi * \text{hour} / 24)$, which maps the 24 hours of the day onto a circle. The same transformation can be applied to other cyclical variables such as day of the week, day of the year, or month.

This sine-cosine encoding technique has several important advantages. First, it preserves the continuity of the cycle, meaning that values close in time remain close in the encoded space. Second, it provides the model with two continuous features that capture the angular relationship of the variable, enabling it to learn temporal patterns more effectively. Third, the transformation is smooth and differentiable, making it particularly well-suited for gradient-based models such as neural networks. By encoding cyclical variables in this way, we allow the model to understand temporal relationships that would be obscured or misrepresented with linear encodings.

The benefit of cyclical encoding becomes particularly evident when analyzing seasonal patterns or recurrent events. In energy demand forecasting, for instance, consumption patterns vary significantly by time of day and day of the week. Encoding these variables with sine and cosine transformations enables the model to learn how demand typically rises during the morning hours and peaks in the evening, regardless of the absolute hour values. Similarly, in e-commerce, purchase behavior might increase during weekends or decrease during late nights. Proper encoding of these cyclical patterns provides the model with a clearer signal, improving accuracy and generalization.

Moreover, cyclical encoding is robust to missing or irregular data, which is common in time series applications. Even if certain hours, days, or months are underrepresented in the training data, the continuous nature of sine and cosine transformations allows the model to interpolate behavior across the cycle. This capability is particularly valuable in forecasting problems, where predictions are made for future periods that may not be fully represented in the historical training set. The model can still learn the overall cyclical structure and apply it to unseen instances.

When implementing cyclical encoding, it is essential to ensure consistent preprocessing across the entire dataset. The range of the variable being encoded must be known and fixed. For example, the hour of the day always ranges from 0 to 23, so the transformation must divide by 24. Any inconsistency in the range used in the sine and cosine calculations can lead to incorrect representations and degrade model performance. It is also important to store the encoding logic so it can be applied consistently during model inference, ensuring that new data is transformed in the same way as the training data.

In practice, cyclical encoding is often used alongside other time-based features to enrich the temporal representation. While sine and cosine encode periodicity, other transformations such as rolling statistics, lag features, or trend indicators can provide additional context. Combining cyclical encoding with these techniques results in a comprehensive time-aware feature set that captures both the repeating nature of time and its evolving patterns. For example, a model predicting web traffic might use sine and cosine transformations for hour and day of the week, rolling averages of past visits, and binary indicators for holidays or special events.

Visualization can help validate the effectiveness of cyclical encoding. Plotting the sine and cosine transformed values over time reveals the smooth periodic wave that mirrors the original cycle. These visualizations also make it easier to identify any anomalies or inconsistencies in the encoding process. Furthermore, examining the learned weights or feature importances associated with the sine and cosine components can offer insights into which time-based cycles are most influential for the model. This interpretability is especially useful in domains where understanding temporal behavior is critical to decision-making.

In summary, cyclical encoding is a crucial technique for faithfully representing time-based variables in machine learning models. It addresses the limitations of linear encoding by respecting the inherent circular structure of time-related data. By mapping cyclical variables to the unit circle using sine and cosine transformations, models can better learn temporal dependencies, capture recurring patterns, and improve predictive performance. Whether applied to hours, days, weeks, or months, cyclical encoding transforms raw timestamps into features that reflect the true nature of time, enabling deeper insights and more accurate models across a wide range of time-sensitive applications.

Feature Engineering from Dates and Timestamps

Dates and timestamps are rich sources of information that often carry far more predictive value than might initially be apparent. They are not just labels marking the moment when an event occurred, but rather containers of temporal signals that can be broken down into multiple informative components. Feature engineering from dates and timestamps involves extracting and transforming these components to reveal patterns related to time. These patterns are especially valuable in time-sensitive applications such as demand forecasting, fraud detection, user behavior analysis, and system monitoring. By decomposing time into its constituent parts and generating derived features, models are given the opportunity to learn from seasonality, trends, periodic behavior, and elapsed intervals that would otherwise remain hidden in a single datetime field.

The first and most common step in date-related feature engineering is the decomposition of the timestamp into discrete units. From a single datetime column, one can extract features such as year, month, week, day, hour, minute, second, day of the week, and day of the year. Each of these components can provide context about the observation that may influence the target variable. For instance, customer behavior may change significantly during weekends compared to weekdays, which makes the day of the week a useful feature. Similarly, transactions that occur in December may exhibit holiday-driven spikes that differ markedly from those in March or July. By splitting timestamps into these granular components, the model can better understand temporal distributions and seasonal variations.

Another valuable transformation is identifying whether a timestamp falls within a particular part of a recurring cycle. This could include features such as whether a date is on a weekend, a public holiday, the end of the month, or during a company-specific promotional period. Boolean features like is_weekend or is_end_of_quarter can help models pick up on time-based thresholds or deadlines that impact human behavior or system activity. These binary indicators are easy to interpret and can be combined with other categorical or numerical features to uncover more complex temporal dynamics. Depending on the business context, additional domain-specific flags can be created, such as is_black_friday or is_back_to_school, capturing industry-relevant time periods that standard calendars do not cover.

Time-based features also provide opportunities to measure the time elapsed between events. Elapsed time features are especially important in transactional systems, where understanding the duration between interactions can offer critical insights. For example, the time since a user's last login or the time since their last purchase can be strong predictors of churn or re-engagement. In financial datasets, the interval between transactions may reveal fraudulent activity if it deviates significantly from a customer's normal pattern. These features often take the form of time deltas measured in seconds, minutes, hours, or days, and they allow the model to consider temporal proximity and urgency.

Time since a reference point is another form of time delta that can be meaningful. This may include the number of days since account creation, the number of hours since a system started recording data, or the time since the beginning of a fiscal quarter. These features help the model understand where an observation sits within a broader timeline, capturing trends over time and highlighting early versus late activity. They are particularly useful for monitoring growth, decay, or engagement trajectories, especially in cohort analysis or lifecycle modeling. When used carefully, these features enable the model to track progressions and detect phase transitions that a flat timestamp would not reveal.

In scenarios involving sessions or user interactions, features related to time of day are especially informative. Converting timestamps into an hour-of-day format helps identify behavioral cycles, such as when users tend to be most active or when certain system events are most likely to occur. For example, in web traffic analytics, peak usage may be concentrated in morning and evening hours, while in transportation data, rush hours define daily patterns. These features can also capture operational cycles, such as machine activity during different shifts or customer service call volumes across the day. Hourly patterns are often tied closely to human behavior, making them highly predictive in user-centric applications.

More advanced forms of date-based feature engineering involve combining multiple time elements into compound features. For example, interactions between the day of the week and hour of the day can be used to model weekly routines. A user visiting a website on Monday at 9 a.m. may exhibit different behavior compared to someone visiting on Friday at the same hour. These compound features can be created manually or discovered through feature interaction techniques, enabling models to learn subtle combinations of time components that drive meaningful variations in the target variable.

Timestamps can also be aligned with external data sources to enhance their informativeness. Weather conditions, public holidays, stock market openings, or major news events can be matched to specific dates and included as additional features. These enrichments help contextualize timestamps with real-world information that may significantly influence outcomes. For instance, temperature and precipitation on a specific date may affect sales of seasonal products, while news sentiment or macroeconomic indicators tied to a date may impact financial trends. Aligning these auxiliary datasets with core timestamps extends the value of date features by grounding them in external context.

Another technique involves encoding cyclical time components using sine and cosine transformations. This method is particularly useful for features such as hour of the day, day of the week, and month of the year, which repeat in a circular pattern. Rather than encoding these variables as linear integers, which can create artificial discontinuities, cyclical encoding places them on a unit circle to reflect their true nature. For example, the hours 23 and 0 are adjacent in time but far apart numerically. By transforming them with sine and cosine functions, models can better capture the continuity of time and improve their understanding of temporal cycles.

Finally, timestamps can serve as the foundation for creating cumulative or rolling statistics. Aggregates such as running averages, rolling sums, or exponentially weighted metrics can be anchored to timestamps to track trends over time. These features are invaluable in time series forecasting, anomaly detection, and trend analysis. By anchoring these rolling features to timestamps, the model gains a dynamic understanding of how key metrics evolve and how the present relates to the recent past. This not only adds temporal depth to the feature set but also helps capture momentum, stability, or deviation patterns that are often pivotal in predictive modeling.

Feature engineering from dates and timestamps is a multifaceted process that transforms raw temporal markers into a structured set of informative variables. These features capture seasonality, cyclicality, event timing, and behavioral patterns, enabling models to make sense of time as a predictive dimension. By carefully extracting, transforming, and enriching date-based features, data scientists empower their models to unlock insights hidden in time and to make accurate, timely, and context-aware predictions.

Extracting Features from Images

Images are a rich and complex form of data, capable of conveying vast amounts of visual information that go far beyond the capacity of traditional structured data. In machine learning, extracting meaningful features from images is a critical step that enables models to interpret, understand, and learn from visual content. Unlike tabular data, where features are already organized into columns with explicit meaning, image data starts as an array of pixel values, often with three color channels for RGB images. To make this data useful for models, it must be transformed into a structured format that captures the underlying patterns, textures, shapes, and semantic information present in the image.

The most basic form of feature extraction from an image involves flattening the pixel array into a one-dimensional vector. For example, a 64x64 RGB image has 64 multiplied by 64 multiplied by 3 values, totaling 12,288 pixel intensities. These values can be directly fed into machine learning models such as support vector machines or logistic regression. However, this approach rarely performs well because raw pixel values are sensitive to noise, lighting conditions, orientation, and background clutter. Moreover, such vectors are extremely high-dimensional and lack the structural information that defines the content of an image.

To address these limitations, traditional computer vision methods apply hand-crafted feature extraction techniques that summarize important visual properties while discarding irrelevant details. One popular approach is the histogram of oriented gradients, or HOG, which captures the distribution of edge directions in localized regions of an image. This technique is particularly effective for detecting objects such as pedestrians, vehicles, or animals, as it encodes the contours and outlines that define shape. Another widely used method is the scale-invariant feature transform, or SIFT, which detects key points in an image and describes them using scale- and rotation-invariant vectors. These descriptors can be matched across images, enabling tasks such as object recognition or image stitching.

Texture-based features, such as local binary patterns, analyze the spatial arrangement of pixel intensities in small neighborhoods. These patterns provide useful representations for applications like facial recognition, fingerprint analysis, or surface inspection in industrial settings. Color histograms, another hand-crafted feature, summarize the distribution of colors within an image and are useful in applications where color plays a dominant role, such as plant species identification or artwork classification. By reducing the high-dimensional pixel space into a lower-dimensional set of descriptive statistics, these methods provide more compact and interpretable features for downstream modeling.

In recent years, the development of deep learning has dramatically changed how features are extracted from images. Convolutional neural networks, or CNNs, are now the standard tool for learning hierarchical representations directly from pixel data. CNNs consist of multiple layers of filters that scan over the image, detecting patterns such as edges, textures, and increasingly complex structures. Early layers of a CNN may detect simple features like lines or corners, while deeper layers combine these into representations of objects, scenes, or concepts. The key advantage of CNNs is their ability to learn relevant features automatically during training, eliminating the need for manual feature design and often outperforming traditional methods.

A common practice in image feature extraction using deep learning is to use a pre-trained CNN as a fixed feature extractor. Models such as VGG, ResNet, Inception, or EfficientNet are trained on massive datasets like ImageNet and can be used to generate feature vectors for new images. This process involves removing the final classification layer of the network and using the outputs of the penultimate layer as the feature representation. These high-level embeddings capture semantic information about the image and are well-suited for tasks such as clustering, similarity search, or transfer learning. Using pre-trained networks allows practitioners to leverage powerful feature extractors without the need for extensive computational resources or labeled data.

Another important approach involves fine-tuning a pre-trained CNN on a specific dataset. Instead of freezing the convolutional layers, the entire model or a subset of layers is retrained on the target task, allowing the network to adapt its learned features to the new domain. This method is particularly useful when the target data is related but not identical to the original training data. Fine-tuning strikes a balance between leveraging prior knowledge and capturing domain-specific patterns, resulting in more accurate and specialized feature representations.

In certain applications, image data is combined with other modalities such as text, audio, or structured data. In these multimodal settings, features extracted from images must be aligned and integrated with features from other sources. For example, in product recommendation systems, image features of clothing items might be combined with textual descriptions, user reviews, and purchase history. Feature extraction pipelines in such scenarios must ensure that the visual embeddings are meaningful and compatible with features from other domains. This often involves normalization, dimensionality reduction, or embedding alignment techniques that bring all modalities into a shared representational space.

Dimensionality reduction is another essential aspect of image feature engineering. While deep networks produce rich and high-dimensional embeddings, working with such large vectors can be computationally expensive and may lead to overfitting. Techniques such as principal component analysis, t-distributed stochastic neighbor embedding, or autoencoders can be applied to compress feature vectors while preserving essential information. These reduced representations are more efficient for storage, faster to process, and can often improve generalization in downstream models.

It is also important to consider spatial information when extracting features from images. While flattening an image destroys spatial relationships between pixels, convolutional architectures preserve this structure, which is critical for tasks that rely on object localization or spatial context. Spatial pyramids, attention mechanisms, and region-based methods like R-CNN further enhance the model's ability to focus on specific parts of the image, extracting localized features that correspond to regions of interest. These techniques are particularly effective in complex scenes where multiple objects are present, or when fine-grained classification is required.

Data augmentation plays a supportive role in feature extraction by increasing the diversity of training examples and encouraging models to learn more robust features. Techniques such as random cropping, flipping, rotation, color jittering, and affine transformations expose the model to variations that it may encounter in real-world settings. Augmentation helps prevent overfitting and encourages the network to focus on invariant properties of the image rather than superficial patterns.

Ultimately, extracting features from images is about capturing the essence of visual content in a form that machine learning models can understand. Whether using traditional techniques like HOG and SIFT, or leveraging the power of deep learning and CNNs, the goal is to represent images in a way that preserves meaningful structure, semantics, and context. Effective image feature engineering transforms raw pixels into powerful representations that unlock the full potential of computer vision in solving real-world problems.

Audio and Signal Processing for Feature Creation

Audio data, like image and text data, contains a wealth of information that is often unstructured and complex. In its raw form, audio is represented as a continuous waveform, a time-series signal that captures changes in air pressure or voltage over time. For machine learning models to interpret and make predictions from audio, this raw signal must be transformed into meaningful and structured features. The process of extracting features from audio relies heavily on signal processing techniques, which help uncover patterns, structures, and characteristics that are not immediately evident in the raw waveform. These features can then be used in tasks such as speech recognition, emotion detection, music classification, acoustic event detection, and even biomedical signal analysis.

The first step in audio feature engineering is often framing and windowing the signal. Since audio signals are continuous and can vary over time, they are typically segmented into short, overlapping frames of a few milliseconds each. Within each frame, the signal is assumed to be stationary, allowing for the application of mathematical transformations that would not be valid over a longer, non-stationary segment. Windowing functions like the Hamming or Hann window are applied to each frame to reduce spectral leakage during analysis. These framed segments serve as the basic units for feature extraction, enabling the model to capture the temporal evolution of the signal.

One of the most common feature sets derived from audio is the set of spectral features, which describe how the energy of the signal is distributed across different frequency components. To obtain these features, the short-time Fourier transform is applied to each windowed frame, converting the signal from the time domain into the frequency domain. This transformation provides a spectrogram, a two-dimensional representation where one axis corresponds to time, the other to frequency, and the intensity represents amplitude. From this spectrogram, several features can be computed, including spectral centroid, spectral bandwidth, spectral contrast, spectral roll-off, and zero-crossing rate. The spectral centroid represents the center of mass of the spectrum and is perceived as the brightness of the sound. The bandwidth measures how spread out the spectrum is, while the roll-off captures the frequency below which a specified percentage of the total energy lies.

Mel-frequency cepstral coefficients, or MFCCs, are among the most widely used audio features in both speech and music analysis. MFCCs are derived from the power spectrum of the signal but are mapped onto a perceptual scale known as the mel scale, which better reflects how humans perceive pitch and frequency. After mapping the spectrum onto the mel scale, a logarithmic transformation is applied, followed by a discrete cosine transform to decorrelate the coefficients. The resulting MFCCs capture the shape of the spectral envelope and provide a compact, fixed-length representation of each audio frame. These features are especially effective in characterizing timbre and vocal tract shape, making them indispensable in automatic speech recognition and speaker identification systems.

Another set of useful features comes from temporal analysis of the audio signal. These features capture properties such as the energy of the signal, the rate of amplitude change, and the distribution of silence and activity over time. Root mean square energy provides a measure of the signal's loudness, while the zero-crossing rate indicates how frequently the waveform changes sign, often corresponding to noisy or high-frequency components. Temporal features are essential in detecting onsets, transients, and rhythmic elements in music, or identifying pauses and speaking rate in speech processing.

For musical applications, chroma features are particularly valuable. These features aggregate the spectral energy into twelve bins corresponding to the twelve semitones of the musical octave. By reducing the influence of timbre and focusing on pitch class, chroma features provide an effective way to capture harmony and chord progressions. They are widely used in music information retrieval tasks such as key detection, genre classification, and audio fingerprinting. In combination with beat tracking and tempo estimation, chroma features enable detailed analysis of the musical structure and rhythmic content of a recording.

Wavelet transforms offer another method for analyzing audio signals. Unlike the Fourier transform, which represents the signal using sine and cosine waves, the wavelet transform uses functions that are localized in both time and frequency. This dual localization allows for the detection of transient events, which are important in non-stationary signals like speech or environmental sounds. Wavelet-based features can reveal sudden changes, clicks, or impacts, and are particularly useful in biomedical applications such as ECG or EEG signal analysis, where brief irregularities may indicate critical health conditions.

Higher-order features can be engineered by aggregating frame-level statistics across entire audio clips. These include mean, variance, skewness, kurtosis, and other statistical descriptors of basic features such as MFCCs or spectral centroids. By summarizing the temporal evolution of features, these statistics provide a global view of the audio content and reduce the dimensionality of the data. Additionally, delta and delta-delta coefficients, which represent the first and second derivatives of MFCCs over time, capture the dynamic behavior of the audio signal, adding temporal context to otherwise static features.

In deep learning workflows, raw waveforms can also be fed directly into neural networks, particularly convolutional or recurrent architectures. These models can learn to extract relevant features automatically, especially when trained on large datasets. However, handcrafted features like MFCCs, chroma, and spectral descriptors remain important due to their interpretability, lower computational requirements, and effectiveness in scenarios with limited data. Pretrained models such as VGGish, which is trained on large-scale audio datasets, can also be used to extract embeddings from audio signals. These embeddings serve as high-level features that capture semantic information and can be fine-tuned for specific tasks such as acoustic scene classification or emotion recognition.

Audio data often contains background noise, artifacts, and inconsistencies due to differences in recording equipment, environment, or user behavior. Preprocessing steps such as noise reduction, silence trimming, and normalization are therefore essential to ensure that extracted features reflect the underlying content rather than irrelevant variability. Techniques like spectral gating, bandpass filtering, and voice activity detection help isolate the informative parts of the signal and improve feature quality.

Ultimately, the goal of audio and signal processing for feature creation is to convert complex and high-dimensional waveforms into structured representations that are informative, compact, and aligned with the modeling objective. Through a combination of temporal, spectral, perceptual, and statistical techniques, audio signals can be transformed into powerful features that allow machine learning models to understand, classify, and generate insights from sound. Whether in voice interfaces, music recommendation systems, healthcare diagnostics, or environmental monitoring, effective audio feature engineering opens the door to intelligent systems that can hear and respond to the world.

Feature Engineering in Graph-Based Data

Graph-based data structures are fundamentally different from traditional tabular datasets. Instead of storing information in rows and columns, graphs represent data as nodes connected by edges, often enriched with attributes on both. These structures naturally model relationships and interactions between entities and are widely used in domains such as social networks, recommendation systems, biological networks, transportation, fraud detection, and knowledge graphs. Feature engineering in graph-based data involves generating informative representations that capture both the properties of individual nodes and the structure of the graph as a whole. This process enables machine learning algorithms to learn from the rich interconnected patterns that define complex systems.

At the core of graph-based feature engineering is the challenge of representing relational information in a numerical format suitable for learning algorithms. Unlike flat data, where each sample is independent, in graphs the value of a node often depends not only on its own attributes but also on the attributes and structure of its neighbors. A simple starting point is to extract node-level features from the raw graph. These may include structural features such as degree, which is the number of connections a node has, or clustering coefficient, which measures how tightly its neighbors are connected. Degree centrality provides an initial insight into how connected a node is, while the clustering coefficient indicates how likely it is that a node's neighbors are also connected, revealing local community structures.

Additional centrality metrics offer more nuanced information. Betweenness centrality captures how often a node appears on the shortest path between other nodes, highlighting its role as a bridge or broker within the network. Closeness centrality measures how close a node is to all other nodes in the graph, offering a sense of reachability. Eigenvector centrality considers not just the quantity of connections but the quality, by giving higher scores to nodes connected to other highly ranked nodes. These features provide insight into the role and influence of nodes within the overall network structure and are often used in social network analysis, citation networks, and financial transaction networks.

Neighborhood aggregation is another key strategy in graph-based feature engineering. It involves summarizing information about a node's local neighborhood to create new features. This can be as simple as computing the average, maximum, or sum of a certain attribute among a node's neighbors. For example, in a product recommendation graph where nodes represent products and edges represent co-purchases, one might compute the average rating of a product's neighbors to estimate its contextual quality. In fraud detection networks, suspicious behavior might be inferred by examining the transaction patterns of connected entities. These aggregated features enable the model to learn not just from the attributes of a node, but from the patterns surrounding it.

Graph-level features can also be engineered to characterize entire networks or subgraphs. This is particularly useful when the task involves classifying or comparing different graphs, such as in cheminformatics, where molecules are represented as graphs of atoms and bonds. Features such as graph diameter, density, number of connected components, and average path length help capture the overall shape and complexity of a graph. These metrics can provide crucial context for classification tasks that involve different types of structures, such as distinguishing between different classes of molecules or identifying abnormal patterns in infrastructure networks.

Edge-level features are equally important in graph-based learning, especially in tasks like link prediction or edge classification. These features describe the relationship between two nodes and often include the number of common neighbors, Jaccard similarity, or the Adamic-Adar score, which weighs rare connections more heavily. These measures are based on the structural overlap of neighborhoods and are used to quantify the strength or likelihood of a connection. In recommender systems, for example, such features help identify potential links between users and items based on shared interactions. Combining these with domain-specific attributes enhances the expressiveness of the graph representation.

Graph embeddings represent a powerful class of techniques that generate dense vector representations of nodes, edges, or entire graphs. These embeddings aim to preserve the structure and semantics of the graph in a lower-dimensional space, enabling traditional machine learning models to operate effectively. Node2Vec and DeepWalk are classic methods that perform random walks on the graph to generate sequences of nodes, which are then used to train embeddings using techniques borrowed from natural language processing. These embeddings capture proximity and structural similarity between nodes, making them useful for tasks such as classification, clustering, and anomaly detection.

Graph convolutional networks have emerged as a transformative approach in learning features directly from graph data. These networks extend the principles of convolution to non-Euclidean structures by aggregating features from a node's neighborhood in a hierarchical manner. The learned features are task-specific and are optimized during training, eliminating the need for manual feature design. Each layer in a graph neural network captures increasingly global context, enabling deep representations of node roles and relationships. Despite their power, these methods still benefit from thoughtful feature engineering, particularly in defining input features and constructing meaningful adjacency structures.

Temporal graphs, where edges or nodes have timestamps, introduce the dimension of time to graph feature engineering. In such graphs, interactions are not static but evolve over time. Feature engineering must then consider not just the presence of a connection, but when and how often it occurred. Features might include edge frequency over time, recency of last interaction, or temporal motifs that capture time-ordered patterns of interactions. These features are particularly valuable in dynamic settings like financial fraud detection, where the timing and sequence of transactions can indicate illicit activity.

Heterogeneous graphs, composed of multiple types of nodes and edges, require specialized feature engineering approaches. In knowledge graphs, for example, entities such as people, organizations, and events are linked by different types of relationships. Feature engineering in this context involves encoding the type and directionality of edges, aggregating features across meta-paths, and capturing semantics through relational embeddings. The diversity of node and edge types adds complexity but also enriches the representational power of the graph, making it possible to model multifaceted systems such as recommendation engines, citation networks, and biological pathways.

Effective feature engineering in graph-based data transforms raw relational structures into powerful representations that unlock the potential of networked systems. By leveraging topological, statistical, and learned features, data scientists can model not only individual entities but also the intricate web of relationships that bind them. Whether through handcrafted metrics, neighborhood aggregation, or deep learning-based embeddings, graph feature engineering provides the foundation for predictive and interpretable machine learning on complex relational data.

Dimensionality Reduction with PCA

In modern data science, datasets often contain an overwhelming number of features. These high-dimensional datasets, while rich in information, can lead to computational inefficiencies, difficulties in visualization, and even degraded model performance due to the curse of dimensionality. One of the most effective techniques to address these challenges is Principal Component Analysis, commonly known as PCA. PCA is a powerful linear dimensionality reduction method that transforms high-dimensional data into a lower-dimensional form while retaining as much of the original variance as possible. It accomplishes this by finding new axes, or principal components, which are linear combinations of the original features and are ordered by the amount of variance they capture from the data.

PCA operates by identifying the directions, or principal components, along which the variance in the data is maximized. These directions are orthogonal to each other and are found by computing the eigenvectors and eigenvalues of the covariance matrix of the data. The eigenvectors represent the directions of maximum variance, while the eigenvalues quantify the amount of variance captured along each direction. By selecting a subset of the top principal components, it is possible to project the data into a lower-dimensional space that preserves the most important structure of the dataset. This projection allows for simpler models, improved performance, and reduced storage requirements.

The process begins by centering the data, subtracting the mean of each feature so that the dataset has zero mean. This step ensures that the first principal component corresponds to the direction of maximum variance rather than being biased by feature offsets. After centering, the covariance matrix is computed to capture how features vary together. The eigenvectors and their corresponding eigenvalues are then extracted from this matrix. These eigenvectors form the new basis for the data, and by selecting the top k eigenvectors based on their eigenvalues, the dimensionality of the data can be reduced from n features to k principal components.

One of the primary benefits of PCA is its ability to uncover latent structure in the data. High-dimensional datasets often contain redundant or correlated features that do not contribute independently to the overall information. PCA reduces this redundancy by transforming correlated features into a smaller set of uncorrelated variables. These principal components are ordered such that the first few capture the most significant variations in the data, allowing for efficient summarization and noise reduction. In many cases, a small number of components can explain a large proportion of the variance, enabling dimensionality reduction without significant loss of information.

PCA is especially useful as a preprocessing step before applying machine learning algorithms. Many algorithms, such as logistic regression, k-means clustering, or support vector machines, can suffer when input features are highly correlated or when the dimensionality is high relative to the number of observations. By reducing dimensionality, PCA improves numerical stability, speeds up training, and can even enhance model performance by eliminating irrelevant or noisy features. It is also frequently used for data visualization, where complex, high-dimensional datasets are projected into two or three dimensions for exploration and interpretation. These visualizations can reveal clusters, trends, or anomalies that would be difficult to detect in the original feature space.

Despite its strengths, PCA has limitations that must be considered when applying it. Because PCA is a linear method, it cannot capture non-linear relationships between features. If the data lies on a non-linear manifold, other techniques such as kernel PCA or t-SNE may be more appropriate. Additionally, the principal components are linear combinations of all input features and often lack interpretability. Unlike the original features, which may have clear semantic meaning, principal components are abstract constructs that represent directions in feature space. This can be a drawback in domains where interpretability is critical, such as healthcare or finance.

Another important consideration is the scaling of input features before applying PCA. Since PCA is based on variance, it is sensitive to the scale of the features. Variables with larger variances will dominate the principal components if the data is not standardized. Therefore, it is standard practice to normalize features to have unit variance before applying PCA. This ensures that all features contribute equally to the analysis and that the resulting components are not biased by differences in scale.

Choosing the number of components to retain is another key decision in PCA. This is typically done by examining the explained variance ratio, which indicates the proportion of the total variance captured by each component. A common approach is to create a scree plot that shows the cumulative explained variance as a function of the number of components. The point at which the curve begins to level off, often called the elbow point, provides a heuristic for selecting an appropriate number of components. Alternatively, a threshold can be set, such as retaining enough components to explain 95 percent of the variance, balancing dimensionality reduction with information preservation.

PCA also supports feature decorrelation, which can be particularly beneficial in statistical modeling. Many models, especially those that rely on assumptions of feature independence or linearity, benefit from inputs that are uncorrelated. By transforming the data into a set of orthogonal components, PCA aligns the data with the axes of maximum variability and removes multicollinearity. This helps models better learn the underlying structure of the data and reduces the risk of overfitting, especially when the number of original features is large.

In some advanced applications, PCA is integrated into pipeline workflows where dimensionality reduction is combined with feature selection, modeling, and evaluation. For example, PCA can be applied during cross-validation to ensure that the dimensionality reduction is fitted only on the training data in each fold, preserving the validity of the evaluation. It can also be used for anomaly detection, where reconstruction error from PCA projection is used to identify outliers that do not conform to the dominant patterns in the data.

Ultimately, PCA is a foundational technique in the feature engineering toolbox, offering a principled way to reduce complexity, improve model efficiency, and uncover structure in high-dimensional datasets. Its mathematical elegance and practical utility make it a go-to method for many data scientists working across a wide array of domains. When applied thoughtfully, PCA enables the transformation of large, noisy, and redundant feature sets into compact and informative representations that enhance both the interpretability and performance of machine learning models.

Feature Selection Using Filter Methods

In machine learning, the quality of features used to train a model often determines the success or failure of the predictive task. As datasets grow larger and more complex, they frequently include redundant, irrelevant, or noisy features that can obscure meaningful patterns, increase training time, and lead to overfitting. Feature selection is the process of identifying and retaining only the most relevant variables from the dataset to improve model performance, reduce complexity, and enhance interpretability. Among the various strategies for feature selection, filter methods are among the most commonly used due to their simplicity, scalability, and model-agnostic nature.

Filter methods work by evaluating the relevance of each feature independently of any specific machine learning model. This is done by computing a statistical score that quantifies the relationship between each feature and the target variable. Features are ranked based on these scores, and a subset of the top-ranked features is selected for further modeling. Because filter methods do not rely on a model to assess feature importance, they are fast, easy to implement, and suitable for high-dimensional datasets. They are especially useful in the early stages of feature selection, where the goal is to quickly eliminate obviously irrelevant variables.

The choice of scoring metric in filter methods depends on the nature of the data and the type of machine learning task. For classification problems with categorical targets, common metrics include chi-squared statistics, mutual information, and ANOVA F-values. The chi-squared test measures the dependence between a feature and the target by comparing observed and expected frequencies in a contingency table. Features with higher chi-squared values are considered more informative. Mutual information, on the other hand, quantifies the amount of shared information between a feature and the target. It captures both linear and non-linear dependencies and is more flexible than the chi-squared test in detecting complex relationships.

ANOVA F-values compare the variance between groups defined by the target variable to the variance within those groups. A higher F-value indicates that the feature discriminates well between different target classes.

For regression problems with continuous targets, metrics like Pearson correlation, mutual information for continuous variables, and variance thresholds are commonly used. Pearson correlation measures the linear relationship between a feature and the target. Features with high absolute correlation values are considered more predictive. However, correlation only captures linear associations, so it may overlook useful features with non-linear relationships. Mutual information again proves useful here because it can capture a broader range of dependencies. Variance thresholding is a simple technique that removes features with very low variance, which are unlikely to provide useful information. Features with near-constant values across the dataset contribute little to the model and can be safely discarded.

Another important aspect of filter methods is redundancy removal. While filter methods excel at identifying individually informative features, they do not automatically account for redundancy among them. It is common for several features to be highly correlated with each other and the target, leading to multicollinearity in the selected subset. To address this, feature selection can be followed by correlation analysis, where pairs of highly correlated features are identified and one from each pair is removed. This helps improve the stability of models, particularly those sensitive to multicollinearity like linear regression or logistic regression.

Filter methods can also be used to construct new features by identifying interactions or combinations of informative variables. While basic filter techniques evaluate features in isolation, more advanced variants explore pairwise or group-wise interactions using metrics like joint mutual information or redundancy-aware relevance measures. These approaches strike a balance between relevance to the target and uniqueness within the feature set. Though computationally more demanding, they lead to richer and more diverse feature subsets that improve model generalization.

One of the strengths of filter methods is their versatility across different datasets and tasks. They are widely used in domains such as genomics, where the number of features can exceed the number of samples by several orders of magnitude. In such high-dimensional spaces, training a model for feature evaluation is computationally prohibitive, making filter methods an ideal choice. By rapidly narrowing down the feature space, they pave the way for more focused and effective modeling efforts. Filter methods are also commonly used in text classification, where thousands of terms extracted from documents must be reduced to a manageable subset before modeling.

Despite their advantages, filter methods must be applied with care. Because they evaluate features independently of the model, they may miss features that are weak on their own but strong in combination with others. Additionally, the thresholds used to select features—such as a fixed number of top features or a minimum score—are often arbitrary and may need to be tuned through cross-validation. It is also important to ensure that the filter method does not introduce data leakage. For example, if the entire dataset is used to compute selection scores before splitting into training and test sets, the selected features may encode information from the test set, leading to overly optimistic evaluation results.

To mitigate these risks, filter methods are often used as part of a broader feature selection pipeline. They can be combined with wrapper or embedded methods that evaluate features in the context of a specific model. A typical workflow might begin with a filter step to eliminate obviously irrelevant features, followed by a wrapper method like recursive feature elimination to fine-tune the subset. This layered approach balances computational efficiency with modeling accuracy and ensures that the final feature set is both relevant and non-redundant.

In practical applications, filter methods are implemented through a variety of tools and libraries, including scikit-learn in Python, which provides functions for univariate selection using chi-squared, ANOVA, and mutual information scores. These implementations make it easy to experiment with different metrics and thresholds and to integrate feature selection into machine learning pipelines. As data volumes and feature counts continue to grow, the importance of effective, efficient, and interpretable feature selection becomes even more pronounced. Filter methods remain a cornerstone technique, enabling data scientists to distill high-dimensional data into meaningful representations that support accurate and reliable machine learning models.

Wrapper Methods for Feature Selection

Wrapper methods for feature selection represent a powerful and model-driven approach to identifying the most relevant features in a dataset. Unlike filter methods, which evaluate features based on intrinsic statistical properties, wrapper methods rely on the performance of a specific machine learning model to guide the selection process. This approach treats feature selection as a search problem, where different subsets of features are evaluated by training and testing a model using each subset, and the best-performing subset is chosen based on some performance metric. Because wrapper methods take the learning algorithm into account, they are generally more accurate and capable of identifying complex interactions between features, although they are also more computationally intensive.

The core idea behind wrapper methods is simple: evaluate a candidate feature subset by training a model using only those features, then assess the model's performance on a validation set. This performance serves as a proxy for the quality of the feature subset. A search algorithm is then used to explore the space of possible feature subsets, trying to find the one that yields the best results. The search can be exhaustive, testing every possible combination of features, but this quickly becomes infeasible for datasets with many features due to the combinatorial explosion of possible subsets. Therefore, heuristic or greedy search strategies are commonly employed to make the process tractable.

One widely used wrapper technique is forward selection. This method starts with an empty set of features and adds one feature at a time. At each step, the algorithm evaluates all features not yet included and selects the one that, when added to the current subset, results in the greatest improvement in model performance. This process continues until no additional features improve the performance or until a specified number of features have been selected. Forward selection is simple and often effective, but it may miss optimal subsets if an important feature only shows its value when combined with others already included later in the process.

Backward elimination operates in the opposite direction. It begins with the full set of features and iteratively removes the least useful one at each step. In each iteration, the algorithm evaluates the model performance after removing each feature in the current set and eliminates the one whose exclusion degrades the model the least or improves it. This process is repeated until no further improvement is possible or until a stopping criterion is met. Backward elimination is especially useful when the starting feature set is relatively small or when most features are expected to be relevant. However, it can be computationally expensive, especially if retraining the model is time-consuming.

Another common method is recursive feature elimination (RFE), which combines elements of both forward and backward strategies. RFE works by training a model on the full set of features, ranking the features based on some measure of importance derived from the model, and then removing the least important feature or group of features. This process is repeated recursively on the reduced set until the desired number of features is reached. RFE is particularly effective when used with models that provide intrinsic feature importance scores, such as decision trees, linear models with coefficients, or support vector machines with weights. The recursive aspect of the algorithm allows it to iteratively refine the selection, often leading to more robust feature sets.

The primary advantage of wrapper methods lies in their ability to capture interactions among features. Some features may not be individually informative but become highly predictive when used in combination. Wrapper methods can uncover these synergies because they evaluate feature subsets in the context of the model's performance. This leads to more accurate and reliable feature selection, particularly in cases where the target variable is influenced by complex, non-linear relationships among multiple predictors. This characteristic makes wrapper methods especially appealing for high-stakes applications such as medical diagnosis, financial forecasting, and fraud detection, where every increment in predictive accuracy is valuable.

Despite their strengths, wrapper methods are computationally demanding. Each evaluation of a feature subset requires training and validating a model, which becomes costly as the number of features and the size of the dataset increase. To manage this complexity, practitioners often use cross-validation during subset evaluation to obtain more reliable performance estimates and avoid overfitting to the training data. Additionally, parallel processing and caching of intermediate results can help accelerate the search process. In practical scenarios, wrapper methods are often used in conjunction with filter methods: an initial filtering step eliminates clearly irrelevant features, and a wrapper method is then applied to the reduced set to fine-tune the selection.

The success of wrapper methods also depends on the choice of learning algorithm. Since the evaluation is based on model performance, different models may prefer different subsets of features. A subset that works well with a decision tree might not be optimal for a logistic regression model. This model-dependence can be a double-edged sword: while it allows the feature selection to be tailored to the specific modeling task, it also means that the selected features may not generalize well if the model type changes. Therefore, the model used for feature selection should ideally be the same as or closely related to the one intended for deployment.

Another important consideration in wrapper methods is the choice of performance metric. Depending on the problem, accuracy, precision, recall, F1 score, area under the ROC curve, or mean squared error might be used to evaluate feature subsets. The metric should align with the ultimate objective of the modeling task to ensure that the selected features contribute to meaningful improvements in performance. Additionally, wrapper methods can be adapted for multi-objective optimization, where the goal is to balance performance with simplicity, penalizing feature sets that are too large or complex.

Wrapper methods for feature selection offer a flexible and powerful approach to identifying the most predictive subset of features. By directly evaluating the impact of features on model performance, they provide high-quality selections that reflect the real predictive structure of the data. While computational cost remains a challenge, advances in hardware, parallel computing, and algorithmic efficiency continue to make wrapper methods increasingly practical for a wide range of applications. When used thoughtfully and in conjunction with other selection techniques, wrapper methods help data scientists build models that are both accurate and interpretable, ensuring that only the most informative features are used to drive decisions.

Embedded Methods for Feature Relevance

Embedded methods for feature relevance offer a balanced and efficient approach to feature selection by incorporating the process of evaluating feature importance directly into the construction of a machine learning model. Unlike filter methods that operate independently of the learning algorithm or wrapper methods that require iterative model training on different feature subsets, embedded methods perform feature selection as part of the model training itself. This tight integration allows embedded methods to assess the contribution of each feature based on how it influences the model's internal parameters, offering both accuracy and computational efficiency. These methods are especially valuable in high-dimensional settings where the number of features may exceed the number of observations, as they help reduce model complexity and mitigate overfitting without introducing the prohibitive costs of wrapper-based searches.

One of the most well-known examples of embedded methods is regularization-based feature selection in linear models. In linear regression or logistic regression, regularization introduces a penalty term to the loss function that discourages the model from assigning large weights to any single feature. The most prominent regularization techniques are L_1 (Lasso) and L_2 (Ridge) regularization. L_1 regularization, in particular, has a unique property that drives some coefficients to exactly zero during the optimization process. This means that features with coefficients reduced to zero are effectively excluded from the model, achieving automatic feature selection. The remaining features are those deemed most relevant by the algorithm, as they have non-zero coefficients that contribute meaningfully to the prediction task.

L_1 regularization has become a widely used tool in scenarios where interpretability and sparsity are desired. For example, in genomics or finance, where thousands of variables may be available, Lasso can help identify the small subset of features that actually influence the outcome. Its ability to produce sparse models makes it attractive not only for feature selection but also for reducing noise and improving generalization. In practice, a hyperparameter known as the regularization strength controls the degree of sparsity. A higher penalty encourages more coefficients to shrink to zero, resulting in fewer features being selected. Tuning this parameter using cross-validation allows for a trade-off between simplicity and predictive power.

Tree-based algorithms represent another powerful category of embedded methods for feature relevance. Decision trees, random forests, and gradient boosting machines inherently evaluate the importance of each feature during the process of tree construction. In a decision tree, features are selected based on their ability to reduce impurity measures such as Gini impurity or information gain. Features that frequently appear near the top of the tree or contribute substantially to splits are considered more important. When an ensemble of trees is built, as in the case of random forests or boosting, the feature importance scores are aggregated across all trees, providing a robust estimate of relevance.

These tree-based feature importance scores are particularly intuitive and useful in practical settings. They allow data scientists to rank features according to how much they contribute to improving predictive accuracy, offering insights into the structure of the data and the relationships between variables. Unlike L_1 regularization, tree-based models can capture non-linear relationships and interactions between features, making them suitable for a wider variety of datasets. Moreover, many modern libraries such as XGBoost, LightGBM, and CatBoost provide built-in functions to extract and visualize feature importance, streamlining the process of identifying which features drive model predictions.

Embedded methods also include techniques that combine the strengths of multiple selection strategies. Elastic Net, for example, is a regularized linear model that incorporates both L_1 and L_2 penalties. This combination allows it to maintain the sparsity-inducing property of Lasso while benefiting from the stability of Ridge regression. In cases where features are highly correlated, Lasso may arbitrarily select one feature from a group and discard the others, leading to unstable results. Elastic Net addresses this by encouraging group selection, where correlated features can be retained together, enhancing model robustness and interpretability.

Another class of embedded methods leverages model-specific heuristics to determine feature relevance during the learning process. For instance, support vector machines with linear kernels provide weight vectors that indicate the direction and magnitude of each feature's influence on the classification boundary. Features with large absolute weights are more influential, and thresholding these weights can yield a subset of relevant features. Similarly, in neural networks, techniques such as weight pruning and dropout can help identify and remove irrelevant connections, indirectly leading to a more compact and feature-efficient representation of the data. While not designed specifically for feature selection, these methods can be adapted to reduce dimensionality as part of model training.

The integration of feature selection into the learning algorithm offers several practical benefits. First, it reduces the need for separate feature engineering steps, simplifying the overall workflow. Second, it ensures that the selected features are aligned with the modeling objective, as their relevance is measured based on the actual optimization of the loss function. Third, embedded methods often result in faster training and inference times due to the reduced number of active features, which is particularly important in real-time systems and resource-constrained environments.

However, embedded methods are not without limitations. Because they depend on the structure and assumptions of the specific model being used, the selected features may not generalize well across different algorithms. For example, features identified as important by a linear model with L1 regularization may differ significantly from those highlighted by a tree-based ensemble. This model dependency can be both a strength and a weakness, depending on whether the final model is known in advance or subject to change. Additionally, while embedded methods are computationally more efficient than wrappers, they still require the model to be retrained during feature selection, which can be time-consuming for large datasets or complex algorithms.

Despite these challenges, embedded methods remain a cornerstone of modern feature selection practice. They offer a compelling balance of interpretability, efficiency, and predictive accuracy, particularly when combined with cross-validation and other validation strategies. As machine learning continues to evolve toward greater automation and integration, embedded methods are poised to play an increasingly central role in model development, enabling more intelligent systems that can identify, prioritize, and learn from the most informative aspects of high-dimensional data. Through their seamless blending of feature relevance assessment with model training, embedded methods empower practitioners to build leaner, faster, and more insightful models across a wide range of applications.

Mutual Information and Correlation Analysis

Understanding the relationships between features and between features and the target variable is a fundamental step in the feature engineering process. Two of the most widely used techniques to explore and quantify these relationships are mutual information and correlation analysis. Both methods provide insights into how variables are related, but they approach the problem from different statistical perspectives and offer complementary benefits. While correlation analysis focuses primarily on linear relationships, mutual information captures a broader spectrum of dependencies, including non-linear associations. By combining these techniques, data scientists can make informed decisions about which features to include, which ones to transform, and which ones to potentially eliminate from a model.

Correlation analysis is a statistical method that measures the strength and direction of a linear relationship between two continuous variables. The most common metric used is Pearson's correlation coefficient, which ranges from -1 to 1. A coefficient close to 1 implies a strong positive linear relationship, while a value near -1 suggests a strong negative linear relationship. A value around zero indicates little to no linear association between the variables. Pearson's correlation is simple to compute and interpret, making it a valuable initial tool for exploratory data analysis. However, it has notable limitations. It assumes a linear relationship and is sensitive to outliers, which can significantly distort the results. If two variables are related in a non-linear way, Pearson's coefficient may fail to capture the true dependency.

To address some of these limitations, other types of correlation measures can be used. Spearman's rank correlation, for instance, assesses the monotonic relationship between two variables by comparing their rank orders. It is less sensitive to outliers and can detect non-linear but monotonic associations. Kendall's tau is another non-parametric measure that evaluates the strength of the association by examining the concordance and discordance between variable pairs. These alternative correlation measures provide greater flexibility in identifying meaningful relationships, especially in datasets that deviate from the assumptions of normality or linearity.

Mutual information, by contrast, originates from information theory and measures the amount of shared information between two variables. It quantifies how much knowing the value of one variable reduces uncertainty about the other. Unlike correlation, mutual information does not assume any specific type of relationship, linear or otherwise. This makes it a powerful tool for detecting both linear and complex non-linear dependencies. Mutual information is always non-negative and equals zero if and only if the variables are completely independent. Higher values indicate stronger associations, regardless of the functional form of the relationship.

Computing mutual information involves estimating the joint probability distribution of the variables involved. For discrete variables, this is straightforward and typically done using frequency counts. For continuous variables, mutual information estimation is more challenging and often requires discretization or the use of kernel density estimation methods. Despite this computational complexity, mutual information offers a robust and flexible way to assess relevance, especially in scenarios where features interact with the target variable in non-obvious ways.

In practical feature selection workflows, both mutual information and correlation analysis serve as valuable filters to reduce dimensionality and improve model efficiency. Features that are highly correlated with the target are likely to be informative, but care must be taken when multiple features are also highly correlated with each other. This multicollinearity can introduce redundancy, inflate model variance, and obscure the individual effects of predictors. Correlation matrices and heatmaps are often used to visualize inter-feature relationships and identify clusters of correlated variables. Once detected, highly correlated features may be consolidated, dropped, or transformed using techniques such as principal component analysis to reduce redundancy.

Mutual information is particularly useful in classification problems where the relationship between categorical features and a categorical target is not captured by traditional correlation metrics. In such cases, mutual information provides a clear quantification of dependency, helping to identify features that contribute to the predictability of class labels. For instance, in a customer churn dataset, mutual information can reveal whether the usage pattern of a specific service strongly influences the likelihood of churn, even if the relationship is non-linear or interacts with other behaviors.

In regression problems, mutual information can also uncover subtle dependencies between numerical features and a continuous target. By discretizing the target variable or using advanced estimators, it becomes possible to identify features that play an important role in explaining variance, even when correlation analysis shows a weak linear association. This capability makes mutual information a powerful complement to correlation, particularly in domains like finance, biology, or sensor data, where relationships are often complex and multi-faceted.

An important aspect of using mutual information and correlation analysis effectively is ensuring that the data is properly prepared. Outliers, missing values, and inappropriate scaling can distort the measurements and lead to incorrect interpretations. Preprocessing steps such as normalization, outlier removal, and imputation should be applied before calculating these statistics. Additionally, mutual information and correlation analysis should be used within the context of the specific modeling goal. Features that are weakly associated with the target might still be valuable if they interact strongly with other features, while strongly correlated features may be irrelevant or misleading in certain domains.

Another consideration is the interpretability of the selected features. Mutual information scores and correlation coefficients provide quantitative evidence of feature relevance, but they do not offer causal explanations. A high mutual information score does not imply that a feature causes changes in the target, only that there is a dependence. Similarly, a high correlation coefficient does not indicate causality. Therefore, domain knowledge, exploratory data analysis, and model-based techniques should also be used to validate and interpret the results of these analyses.

Ultimately, mutual information and correlation analysis are essential tools for feature selection and engineering. They offer complementary strengths, with correlation providing quick insights into linear associations and mutual information capturing broader patterns of dependency. When used together, they enable data scientists to gain a deeper understanding of the structure and relationships within their data, guiding the creation of features that enhance model accuracy, stability, and interpretability. These techniques help distill large, noisy datasets into focused, informative subsets that power effective machine learning pipelines and intelligent decision-making.

Dealing with Multicollinearity in Features

Multicollinearity occurs when two or more features in a dataset are highly correlated, meaning they contain similar information about the variance in the target variable. This phenomenon is particularly problematic in linear models, where it can inflate the variance of coefficient estimates, reduce model interpretability, and lead to unstable predictions. Multicollinearity does not necessarily impact the overall predictive power of a model, but it poses serious issues for understanding the role and importance of individual predictors. Detecting, diagnosing, and addressing multicollinearity is therefore an essential part of the feature engineering and modeling process, especially in scenarios where transparency and coefficient interpretation are critical.

One of the first signs of multicollinearity in a model is the presence of large standard errors for regression coefficients. When predictors are highly correlated, the model struggles to assign unique importance to each one, resulting in coefficients that may fluctuate significantly with small changes in the data. These unstable estimates make it difficult to determine the true relationship between each predictor and the target variable. In extreme cases, the signs of the coefficients may even be counterintuitive or opposite to what domain knowledge would suggest. This undermines the trustworthiness of the model and complicates any efforts to derive actionable insights from it.

To identify multicollinearity, analysts often begin by examining the correlation matrix of the features. This matrix reveals pairwise correlations between variables, and high absolute values close to one indicate strong linear relationships. However, pairwise correlation only captures bivariate associations and may miss more complex multivariate collinearity. For a more comprehensive diagnosis, the variance inflation factor, or VIF, is used. The VIF quantifies how much the variance of a regression coefficient is inflated due to the presence of multicollinearity. A VIF of one indicates no correlation with other features, while higher values suggest increasing levels of multicollinearity. As a general rule of thumb, a VIF above 5 or 10 is considered problematic, though the threshold may vary depending on the context.

Once multicollinearity has been detected, there are several strategies to address it. One of the simplest approaches is to remove one of the correlated features. When two variables provide nearly identical information, dropping one can eliminate the redundancy without sacrificing predictive power. This method is effective when domain knowledge indicates that one of the features is less relevant, harder to measure, or more costly to collect. However, care must be taken to ensure that the retained feature captures the necessary information for the model to perform well.

Another approach involves combining the correlated features into a single new variable. This can be done using mathematical transformations such as taking the average, sum, or difference of the features. In some cases, dimensionality reduction techniques like principal component analysis (PCA) are used to transform the correlated features into a smaller set of uncorrelated components. PCA achieves this by projecting the original data onto a new set of orthogonal axes that capture the maximum variance. The resulting components can then be used as inputs to the model, eliminating multicollinearity while retaining most of the original information. Although PCA reduces multicollinearity, it may compromise interpretability since the principal components are linear combinations of the original variables and do not have straightforward meanings.

Regularization techniques offer another powerful method for dealing with multicollinearity, particularly when the goal is to build a predictive model rather than to interpret coefficients. Lasso regression, which uses L_1 regularization, tends to shrink the coefficients of less relevant or redundant features to zero, effectively performing variable selection and reducing multicollinearity. Ridge regression, which applies L_2 regularization, does not eliminate coefficients but instead penalizes their magnitude, leading to more stable estimates in the presence of multicollinearity. Elastic Net, which combines L_1 and L_2 penalties, offers a balance between variable selection and coefficient shrinkage and is particularly useful when predictors are highly correlated.

Centering and scaling the data is also a common preprocessing step when dealing with multicollinearity, especially in regularized models.

Centering subtracts the mean from each feature, while scaling adjusts features to have unit variance. This transformation does not eliminate multicollinearity, but it improves numerical stability and ensures that the regularization penalties are applied consistently across features. In linear models, centering and scaling also help make the interpretation of coefficients more meaningful and reduce the impact of feature magnitude on model estimation.

In domain-specific applications, multicollinearity can be addressed by rethinking the feature engineering process altogether. For example, in economic models, GDP per capita and income might be strongly correlated. Instead of including both, an analyst might choose to use a derived variable like income inequality or purchasing power index that provides more unique information. Similarly, in marketing analytics, including both the total number of customers and the number of active customers might introduce multicollinearity. In such cases, computing the proportion of active customers as a new variable could reduce redundancy and enhance interpretability.

In time series datasets, multicollinearity often arises from lagged variables and trend-related features. For instance, including multiple lagged values of the same variable can lead to high correlation between those lags. To manage this, analysts can conduct autocorrelation and partial autocorrelation analyses to identify the most informative lags and exclude those that contribute little additional value. Stationarizing the data by differencing or detrending can also help reduce correlation between sequential observations, improving the model's ability to extract meaningful patterns.

Feature selection techniques based on mutual information or model-based importance scores can also help mitigate multicollinearity by prioritizing features that contribute unique information. These methods evaluate the relevance of features to the target variable while accounting for interactions and redundancy. Recursive feature elimination, forward selection, and embedded methods using tree-based models or penalized regressions can identify subsets of features that optimize model performance while reducing collinearity.

Ultimately, dealing with multicollinearity is not about blindly removing correlated variables but about making informed choices that balance model simplicity, interpretability, and predictive accuracy. Each method has trade-offs, and the best approach depends on the specific modeling goals, the type of algorithm being used, and the characteristics of the dataset. In interpretive models like linear regression, reducing multicollinearity is essential to ensure that coefficient estimates are meaningful and stable. In predictive models, the focus may shift toward using regularization or dimensionality reduction to preserve performance while managing feature interactions. A thoughtful strategy for handling multicollinearity allows data scientists to create models that are not only accurate but also robust, interpretable, and aligned with the practical needs of their applications.

Creating Interaction Features for Nonlinear Models

Interaction features are a powerful mechanism in the process of feature engineering, allowing models to capture the effects that arise when two or more features influence the target variable in a combined or interdependent way. In many real-world problems, the relationship between input variables and the target is not purely additive. Instead, the impact of one variable may depend on the level or presence of another, which introduces a form of complexity that linear models cannot naturally capture unless interaction terms are explicitly included. For nonlinear models, especially tree-based methods, gradient boosting machines, and neural networks, interaction features can further enhance performance by explicitly guiding the model to examine combinations of variables that are known or suspected to be important based on domain knowledge or data exploration.

Nonlinear models, by design, have the capacity to capture interactions implicitly. For instance, decision trees can model feature interactions through their hierarchical splitting process, where splits on one feature are conditioned on previous splits on other features. Similarly, neural networks can approximate arbitrary nonlinear functions given enough depth and data, inherently modeling interactions through their layered structure. However, even with such modeling power, providing well-constructed interaction features can make these models more efficient, reduce the burden of learning complex patterns from scratch, and lead to better generalization. Moreover, incorporating interaction terms explicitly allows for better interpretability, as it becomes possible to trace how specific combinations of features affect the outcome.

Creating interaction features involves combining two or more existing features into a new feature that represents their joint effect. The most straightforward way to create an interaction feature is to multiply two features together. For instance, in a marketing dataset, multiplying advertising spend by number of impressions can capture a combined impact that neither variable alone conveys effectively. Such multiplicative interactions are particularly useful when the individual variables have a compounding or synergistic effect on the target. In contrast, additive or difference-based interactions, such as adding or subtracting one feature from another, can highlight relative relationships or dependencies, such as comparing two numerical scores or measuring deviation from a benchmark.

Categorical features can also be involved in interaction terms. When dealing with one-hot encoded variables, interactions can be formed by combining specific categories into new composite categories. For example, if one feature is customer region and another is product type, combining the two into a new feature representing region-product pairs might reveal preferences or behavior patterns unique to certain segments. These types of interactions often prove valuable in personalization systems, where different combinations of user attributes and contextual variables determine outcomes like recommendations or pricing. However, care must be taken when constructing categorical interactions, especially in high-cardinality scenarios, as the number of possible combinations can grow rapidly and lead to sparsity and overfitting.

Interaction features are particularly helpful in domains where known domain relationships exist between variables. In physics, finance, healthcare, and engineering, there are often well-established functional relationships between variables that can be incorporated into models through interaction terms. For example, in epidemiological modeling, the effect of a treatment might depend on both dosage and duration, suggesting an interaction between these two variables. In credit scoring, the risk associated with income may change depending on the level of debt, and the ratio of debt to income is a classic example of a meaningful interaction feature. Encoding such relationships into the model structure can significantly improve its ability to learn relevant patterns.

Another approach to generating interaction features involves statistical or algorithmic methods. Techniques such as polynomial feature expansion systematically generate all pairwise or higher-order combinations of features up to a specified degree. These features can then be evaluated using regularization-based models like Lasso or Elastic Net, which help select only the most relevant interactions. Decision trees can also be used to identify potentially useful interactions by analyzing which features appear together in splits across different paths. Feature importance or SHAP interaction values derived from tree-based models can highlight pairs of variables that interact strongly in the predictive process, providing guidance on which interactions to consider explicitly.

While interaction features offer substantial modeling benefits, they also come with risks. The addition of many interaction terms increases the dimensionality of the dataset, which can lead to overfitting, particularly in small or noisy datasets. This necessitates careful regularization, cross-validation, and potentially feature selection to retain only those interactions that improve model performance. It is also important to remember that not all feature interactions are meaningful or helpful. Blindly generating interactions without a theoretical or empirical basis can introduce noise, inflate model complexity, and reduce interpretability. Therefore, interaction feature creation should ideally be guided by a combination of domain expertise and data-driven evidence.

In the context of feature selection, interaction terms often exhibit lower marginal importance compared to main effects, but their inclusion can significantly enhance the model when they align with important joint behaviors. To evaluate the contribution of interaction features, it is useful to track performance metrics with and without them during model development. If the inclusion of an interaction term leads to a notable improvement in accuracy, precision, recall, or other relevant metrics, this provides evidence of its utility. Techniques like permutation importance or SHAP interaction values offer further insights into the role of these features in complex models.

Visualization can also play a key role in understanding and validating interaction features. For numeric features, plotting the partial dependence of the target on one variable at different levels of another can reveal interaction effects. Heatmaps, surface plots, or stratified line plots can visually highlight how the relationship between one predictor and the outcome changes based on another predictor. These visual tools not only aid in feature engineering but also enhance the interpretability and explainability of the final model, which is particularly important in regulated industries or high-stakes decision-making environments.

Creating interaction features for nonlinear models is a sophisticated and valuable step in the modeling pipeline. While nonlinear algorithms may be capable of modeling complex relationships on their own, providing them with well-chosen interaction terms can accelerate learning, improve performance, and offer deeper insights into the data. These features help bridge the gap between raw data and the functional dependencies that truly drive outcomes, enabling models to act not only as predictors but also as interpretable tools that reveal the intricate connections underlying real-world phenomena. Through a thoughtful balance of theory, data exploration, and algorithmic support, interaction feature engineering remains one of the most impactful techniques for building robust, expressive, and insightful predictive systems.

Polynomial Feature Generation

Polynomial feature generation is a powerful and widely used technique in feature engineering that aims to capture nonlinear relationships between variables by introducing new features based on polynomial combinations of the original ones. This method expands the feature space by including not only the original features but also their higher-order powers and interactions. By enriching the dataset with these polynomial terms, models can learn more complex patterns that linear representations may fail to capture. Polynomial features are particularly valuable when using models that are inherently linear, such as linear regression or logistic regression, since they enable these models to fit nonlinear relationships without changing the underlying algorithm.

The process of polynomial feature generation begins with a set of input features, and through mathematical expansion, it creates additional features that represent the square, cube, or higher powers of each variable. It also includes interactions between features, such as the product of two or more distinct features. For instance, given two input features x and y, polynomial expansion of degree two would yield x, y, x^2, y^2, and xy. The number of features grows rapidly with the degree of the polynomial and the number of input variables. For a dataset with n features and polynomial degree d, the number of generated features can be calculated using a combinatorial formula, which illustrates the exponential growth of the feature space.

The inclusion of polynomial features can significantly improve model performance when the relationship between the input variables and the target variable is nonlinear. In scenarios where a curve or surface better represents the underlying data pattern, these features allow a model that typically learns linear boundaries to approximate curved decision regions. For example, a dataset with a parabolic trend cannot be accurately modeled by a straight line, but adding a squared term allows a linear model to fit the data well. Similarly, interaction terms can reveal dependencies between variables that are only meaningful when considered jointly. These interaction features often play a critical role in domains like finance, physics, and medicine, where variables rarely act in isolation.

However, while polynomial feature generation increases the expressive power of a model, it also introduces challenges. The most immediate concern is the curse of dimensionality. As the number of features increases, especially with higher polynomial degrees, the feature space becomes sparser and more complex. This can lead to overfitting, where the model learns noise in the training data instead of generalizable patterns. Overfitting reduces the model's ability to perform well on unseen data and is particularly problematic in small or noisy datasets. To mitigate this risk, regularization techniques such as Lasso or Ridge regression are commonly used in conjunction with polynomial features. These techniques penalize large coefficients and help ensure that the model remains generalizable.

Computational efficiency is another challenge in polynomial feature generation. The increased number of features leads to higher memory usage and longer training times, especially for algorithms that scale poorly with dimensionality. Feature selection techniques may be necessary to identify and retain only the most informative polynomial terms. Alternatively, one might use domain knowledge to selectively generate only those higher-order terms that are known or suspected to be relevant, avoiding a full combinatorial expansion. For instance, in a mechanical engineering application, a specific product of force and displacement might be known to be critical, while other higher-order combinations are irrelevant and can be excluded.

Despite these concerns, polynomial feature generation remains highly useful, particularly when paired with careful model tuning and validation. Cross-validation is an essential tool for evaluating whether the addition of polynomial features genuinely improves performance. By comparing models trained with and without polynomial features on different validation folds, it becomes possible to quantify their contribution and avoid overfitting. In some cases, a simple second-degree polynomial expansion may yield significant gains without the complexity and cost of deeper expansions. This incremental approach allows practitioners to balance model complexity against interpretability and performance.

Interpretability is another important aspect to consider when using polynomial features. As the model becomes more complex with the inclusion of interaction and power terms, it becomes harder to explain how individual features contribute to the final prediction. In fields where transparency is essential, such as healthcare or finance, the use of polynomial features must be justified and carefully explained. One strategy is to use visualization tools, such as partial dependence plots, to illustrate the effect of individual features and their combinations. Another is to analyze the coefficients in a regularized model to see which polynomial terms are assigned significant weights and contribute meaningfully to predictions.

Polynomial features are not limited to regression tasks; they can also be beneficial in classification problems. When the boundary between classes is nonlinear, adding polynomial terms can help linear classifiers such as logistic regression create curved decision boundaries that better separate the data. This is especially helpful in low-dimensional settings, where visualization can confirm the improved separation provided by polynomial terms. In high-dimensional classification problems, polynomial expansion may still be useful but requires additional precautions to prevent overfitting and ensure model stability.

The generation of polynomial features can also be combined with other feature engineering techniques for even greater effect. For example, after creating polynomial features, one might apply dimensionality reduction techniques such as principal component analysis to reduce the feature space while retaining the essential variance. Alternatively, combining polynomial features with domain-specific transformations or binning strategies can uncover deeper insights into the data and produce more robust models. In automated machine learning pipelines, polynomial feature generation is often included as an optional preprocessing step, with hyperparameters controlling the maximum degree of expansion and the inclusion of interaction terms.

In conclusion, polynomial feature generation offers a simple yet effective way to enhance the capacity of models to learn complex, nonlinear relationships in the data. By systematically introducing higher-order and interaction terms, this technique extends the capabilities of linear models and contributes to the discovery of more accurate, expressive, and insightful models. While care must be taken to manage the risks of overfitting, computational cost, and reduced interpretability, the thoughtful application of polynomial features remains a valuable tool in the data scientist's arsenal, especially when paired with strong validation strategies and regularization techniques.

Target Encoding for High-Cardinality Variables

High-cardinality categorical variables present a significant challenge in feature engineering for machine learning. These variables can take on a large number of unique values, often numbering in the hundreds, thousands, or more. Examples include user IDs, product SKUs, ZIP codes, IP addresses, and URLs. Traditional encoding methods like one-hot encoding become impractical in these cases, as they generate extremely sparse and high-dimensional matrices that are computationally expensive and prone to overfitting. To address this challenge, target encoding has emerged as an effective strategy for transforming high-cardinality categorical variables into numerical representations that preserve useful information while maintaining tractability for machine learning algorithms.

Target encoding, also known as mean encoding or likelihood encoding, replaces each category in a categorical variable with a statistic derived from the target variable. In its simplest form, this involves computing the mean of the target variable for each category and using this value as the encoded feature. For example, in a binary classification task, the proportion of positive labels for each category can serve as its encoded value. This technique transforms categorical variables into meaningful continuous features that directly reflect their relationship with the target. Unlike one-hot encoding, target encoding produces a single numeric column per categorical variable, significantly reducing dimensionality.

One of the primary advantages of target encoding is its ability to retain the predictive power of high-cardinality variables without exploding the feature space. In many cases, certain categories carry strong signals related to the target. For instance, in a retail dataset, some product IDs may have historically high return rates, while others may be consistently associated with high customer satisfaction. Encoding such variables with their target-related statistics preserves these patterns, allowing the model to leverage them effectively. This encoding technique is especially useful for tree-based models like gradient boosting machines, which can interpret numerical values well and do not require feature scaling.

However, despite its power, target encoding introduces a serious risk of data leakage and overfitting if not handled properly. Since the encoding uses information from the target variable, care must be taken to avoid using the entire dataset when computing the means. If the mean for each category is calculated using all available data, the encoding inadvertently includes information from the test set, leading to inflated performance metrics and poor generalization. To prevent this, the encoding should be computed using cross-validation techniques. One common method is to use K-fold cross-validation, where for each fold, the target mean for a category is computed using only the data from the other folds. This ensures that the encoding is based solely on out-of-fold data, preserving the integrity of the training process.

Another approach to mitigating overfitting in target encoding is smoothing. When a category has very few observations, the raw target mean can be highly volatile and may not accurately represent the true relationship between the category and the target. To address this, smoothing techniques blend the category-specific mean with the global mean of the target variable. The degree of blending depends on the frequency of the category, with rare categories relying more on the global mean and frequent categories leaning more heavily on their own target statistics. This Bayesian-style smoothing produces more stable and reliable encodings, particularly when dealing with sparse categories.

In addition to mean encoding, variations of target encoding can be used depending on the nature of the problem. For regression tasks, the mean of the continuous target variable for each category is commonly used. For binary classification, the probability of the positive class serves as the encoded value. For multiclass classification problems, multiple target-encoded features can be created, one for each class. Each of these encodes the probability of the respective class given the category, allowing the model to distinguish between multiple outcome classes. This approach, while more complex, provides a rich representation of high-cardinality features in multiclass settings.

Target encoding can also be extended to incorporate additional statistical measures beyond the mean. Variance, standard deviation, or quantiles of the target variable within each category can provide complementary information and help models capture nuances in the data. These extensions are particularly useful when the distribution of the target within categories is skewed or multimodal. By capturing more than just the central tendency, the encoding becomes more expressive and informative for downstream models.

When using target encoding, it is also important to consider the temporal or hierarchical structure of the data. In time series applications, encoding should be done in a way that respects the chronological order of the data. For example, the target mean for a category at a given time should be computed only from past data, never future data. This rolling target encoding ensures that the model does not access information from the future, which would lead to unrealistic performance in deployment. Similarly, in hierarchical datasets such as those involving products nested within categories, encoding can be applied at multiple levels of aggregation to capture patterns across different granularities.

Interpretability is another benefit of target encoding. Because the encoded values are derived from the target variable itself, they are directly related to the outcome and can be easily understood. For instance, a product category with a high encoded value in a fraud detection model likely corresponds to a higher rate of fraudulent activity. This makes the model's reasoning more transparent and aligns well with domain expert intuition. Target encoding therefore supports not only predictive accuracy but also the interpretability and explainability of the model, which are increasingly important in regulated industries.

In practice, target encoding is often implemented within preprocessing pipelines using popular machine learning libraries. Careful design of these pipelines ensures that the encoding logic is consistent between training and inference, and that the risk of leakage is controlled. Libraries such as category_encoders in Python offer built-in implementations of target encoding with options for smoothing, noise addition, and cross-validation. These tools make it easier to apply target encoding robustly and systematically as part of a larger modeling workflow.

Overall, target encoding provides an elegant solution for handling high-cardinality categorical variables, transforming them into compact, informative, and interpretable features. When applied thoughtfully, with appropriate safeguards against overfitting and leakage, it can unlock the predictive potential of categorical data that would otherwise be lost or poorly represented through conventional encoding methods. Its ability to reduce dimensionality, preserve signal, and enhance model interpretability makes it an indispensable technique in the feature engineering toolkit for both classification and regression problems across a wide range of domains.

Hashing Tricks and Memory-Efficient Representations

As datasets continue to grow in size and complexity, especially in applications like text mining, clickstream analysis, recommendation systems, and web-scale machine learning, memory-efficient representations become increasingly essential. One of the most widely adopted strategies for managing high-dimensional and sparse data is the hashing trick, a technique that maps categorical or token-based data into a fixed-size numerical vector using a hash function. This approach provides a compact and scalable representation without the need to maintain a full dictionary or index of unique values, which can become prohibitively large in high-cardinality scenarios. The hashing trick enables efficient storage and computation, making it a foundational technique in streaming data processing and large-scale machine learning pipelines.

The hashing trick operates by applying a hash function to a categorical value, such as a word or token, and using the resulting hash value to determine the index in a fixed-size feature vector where that token's count or weight should be stored. Instead of creating a separate column for each unique token, as in one-hot encoding or count vectorization, all tokens are projected into a single vector of predefined length. If two different tokens happen to hash to the same index, their values are combined, resulting in a collision. While collisions introduce a small amount of noise, this trade-off is often acceptable given the significant savings in memory and processing time, especially when the number of dimensions is large enough to keep collision probability low.

This method is particularly powerful when dealing with data that cannot be easily pre-enumerated or when the vocabulary is too large to fit into memory. For example, in natural language processing, it is common to encounter millions of distinct n-grams or tokens. Maintaining a dictionary of all possible terms requires substantial memory and slows down feature extraction due to frequent dictionary lookups. The hashing trick eliminates this overhead by using a stateless and deterministic hash function, enabling fast and parallelized transformation of raw inputs into usable features. Because the hash function is consistent, the same input will always be mapped to the same position, making it compatible with online learning and streaming data scenarios.

An important design consideration when using the hashing trick is the choice of hash space size, that is, the number of dimensions in the resulting feature vector. A larger hash space reduces the probability of collisions but increases memory usage. Conversely, a smaller hash space conserves memory but may suffer from a higher collision rate, potentially degrading model performance. In practice, this parameter is chosen based on the available resources and the nature of the data. Empirical testing and cross-validation can help identify the optimal trade-off between accuracy and efficiency. Some implementations even allow the hash size to be dynamically adjusted or tested across multiple configurations in hyperparameter tuning routines.

Another variant of the hashing trick includes the signed hashing trick, in which an additional hash function is used to determine the sign of the value inserted into the feature vector. Instead of simply counting occurrences or assigning weights, the signed hashing approach adds or subtracts values depending on the result of the secondary hash. This technique helps mitigate the effect of collisions by reducing the likelihood that values from unrelated tokens consistently bias the same index in the same direction. By adding this layer of randomness, the signed hashing trick can improve the quality of the approximation and enhance the robustness of downstream models.

Beyond categorical encoding, hashing-based techniques are also used in other forms of memory-efficient data representation. One example is feature hashing for numerical and textual data, where sparse inputs are compressed into fixed-size vectors using random projections. In locality-sensitive hashing (LSH), similar items are mapped to the same hash bucket with high probability, enabling efficient approximate nearest neighbor searches. This is especially useful in large-scale recommendation systems, where fast similarity computations are needed to match users with products or content. Hashing also plays a key role in bloom filters and count-min sketches, which are probabilistic data structures used for set membership testing and frequency estimation in streaming contexts with constrained memory.

Hashing is not limited to preprocessing. It can also be integrated into model architectures. In deep learning, hashed embeddings are used to represent categorical variables when the number of categories is extremely large. Instead of learning separate embeddings for each category, which would consume significant memory, categories are hashed into a smaller embedding table. This technique has been applied successfully in ad click prediction, search ranking, and real-time personalization systems, where embedding tables with millions or billions of entries would be impractical to store and update. By reducing the dimensionality through hashing, these models remain feasible and performant at scale.

Despite its many advantages, hashing does come with limitations. The most prominent issue is the potential for collisions, which can lead to degraded model performance if important distinctions between tokens are lost. In some cases, domain knowledge may dictate that specific tokens or categories should not be merged, and in such cases, traditional encoding methods or custom embeddings may be preferable. Additionally, hashed representations are not human-interpretable, which can be a drawback in applications that require transparency or explainability. For tasks where interpretability is critical, such as healthcare or finance, hashed features may need to be used in conjunction with more interpretable ones or accompanied by post-hoc explanation techniques.

Nevertheless, in large-scale systems where speed, scalability, and memory efficiency are top priorities, hashing remains an invaluable tool. Its simplicity, versatility, and compatibility with distributed systems make it particularly well-suited for modern machine learning pipelines that operate over massive and fast-changing datasets. Frameworks such as Apache Spark, TensorFlow, and scikit-learn provide built-in support for hashing vectorizers and hashed embeddings, making it easy for practitioners to incorporate these techniques into production workflows. Whether used for feature transformation, dimensionality reduction, or similarity estimation, hashing continues to play a critical role in enabling scalable and high-performance machine learning systems.

The strategic use of hashing tricks and memory-efficient representations not only reduces computational overhead but also opens the door to processing data at a scale that would otherwise be infeasible. By embracing probabilistic and approximate methods grounded in robust mathematical principles, data scientists can build models that are both fast and surprisingly accurate, even when working under stringent resource constraints. In a world where data volume is growing exponentially, such techniques are not just helpful but necessary for the next generation of intelligent systems.

Domain Knowledge in Feature Engineering

Feature engineering is often regarded as the art of creating relevant and informative variables that enhance the performance of machine learning models. While algorithmic techniques, statistical tests, and automated tools play a significant role in this process, the power of domain knowledge cannot be overstated. Domain knowledge refers to the expertise and contextual understanding of the specific area from which the data is derived. It enables data scientists to go beyond raw data and uncover features that truly reflect the underlying mechanics of the problem. Integrating domain knowledge into feature engineering results in features that are not only more meaningful and interpretable but also more predictive, offering a decisive advantage in many real-world applications.

The influence of domain knowledge begins at the earliest stage of data exploration. By understanding the origin, structure, and purpose of the dataset, domain experts can identify which variables are likely to be most relevant, which relationships matter, and what forms of data transformation may yield useful insights. In healthcare, for example, a clinician might know that age, blood pressure, and cholesterol levels interact in specific ways that influence patient outcomes. This insight can guide the creation of features such as age-adjusted blood pressure indices or risk scores that combine multiple measurements. Without such knowledge, a purely data-driven approach may overlook these nuanced relationships or fail to capture them in a way that aligns with real-world mechanisms.

In many cases, domain knowledge enables the construction of composite features that reflect meaningful constructs within the field. In finance, the debt-to-income ratio, return on investment, and interest coverage ratio are all examples of engineered features derived from raw financial data. These ratios encapsulate complex economic relationships that are known to influence financial stability, profitability, and creditworthiness. By embedding these relationships into features, models are better equipped to predict outcomes such as default risk, investment success, or corporate health. Similarly, in manufacturing, engineers may use their understanding of machine performance and failure modes to generate features like vibration thresholds, mean time between failures, or rate of temperature change, all of which provide deeper insight than raw sensor readings alone.

Temporal features provide another area where domain expertise adds value. Understanding seasonal cycles, business calendars, and operational workflows enables the transformation of time-based data into features that capture patterns invisible to generic time encodings. In retail, sales patterns may vary significantly between weekdays and weekends or during promotional events and holidays. Rather than relying solely on timestamps, a domain-aware engineer might create binary indicators for sale periods, features for days since last promotion, or cumulative sales for a current campaign. These transformations incorporate the temporal logic of the industry and produce features that are more aligned with the behaviors that affect the target variable.

Spatial data also benefits from domain knowledge. In logistics, real estate, or urban planning, location-based features often drive the most critical decisions. While latitude and longitude are technically sufficient to describe a point in space, they rarely offer intuitive insights to a model. A domain expert might instead suggest features such as distance to the nearest warehouse, classification of urban versus rural zones, proximity to main roads, or inclusion within a specific delivery region. These features simplify complex geospatial relationships into structured, interpretable inputs that retain key context and improve model understanding.

Domain knowledge is particularly important when working with anomalies or edge cases. In some datasets, certain values may appear unusual or extreme but are in fact valid and meaningful under specific conditions. A meteorologist, for instance, might recognize that a sudden temperature spike in a dataset corresponds to a rare atmospheric event rather than an error. Rather than discarding such data as noise, a domain-informed approach might create features that flag these events or encode their duration and intensity. In fraud detection, certain transaction patterns may appear suspicious from a purely statistical perspective, but a fraud analyst could recognize them as legitimate behavior under specific customer profiles or regulatory conditions.

Another benefit of incorporating domain knowledge is the ability to detect and correct errors or inconsistencies in the data. Experts familiar with the domain can identify unrealistic combinations of values, units that have been incorrectly recorded, or anomalies caused by system malfunctions. By flagging and addressing these issues during feature engineering, they ensure the dataset is more accurate and reliable, leading to better model performance and more trustworthy predictions. Domain experts can also inform imputation strategies for missing values, advising on whether certain gaps should be filled, left blank, or replaced with a domain-specific default.

Feature scaling, normalization, and transformation are also areas where domain knowledge plays a critical role. In some fields, variables must be interpreted on a logarithmic or exponential scale due to their natural distribution or impact. A biologist might know that enzyme activity follows a nonlinear curve, while an economist might suggest that income or population size be log-transformed to reflect diminishing returns. Recognizing when and how to apply these transformations requires not only statistical intuition but also an understanding of how the variable behaves in the real world. These transformations help models better approximate the true functional form of the data and often improve both fit and interpretability.

Importantly, domain knowledge supports the generation of features that are interpretable to end users. In many applications, stakeholders must be able to understand and act on model predictions. A model that uses opaque or arbitrary features may be less valuable than one built on domain-grounded inputs that can be explained, validated, and trusted. In regulated industries, such as healthcare, finance, and public safety, explainability is not optional but a legal and ethical requirement. Features that align with domain-specific metrics, standards, or thresholds help bridge the gap between model output and decision-making.

Ultimately, while data-driven methods like automated feature generation, deep learning, and ensemble models continue to advance the field of machine learning, domain knowledge remains a cornerstone of effective feature engineering. It brings context, intuition, and insight that no algorithm can infer on its own. The best models are often those that combine the predictive power of machine learning with the wisdom of human expertise. By embedding domain knowledge into the feature engineering process, data scientists create models that not only perform well but also align with the real-world systems they are meant to support, offering results that are not just accurate but also actionable, trustworthy, and robust.

Feature Engineering in E-Commerce Data

E-commerce platforms generate vast and diverse amounts of data across multiple channels, including website interactions, product catalogs, customer profiles, transaction histories, reviews, search queries, and marketing campaigns. This data, while rich in information, is also highly complex and often unstructured, requiring thoughtful transformation into structured formats that can be used effectively by machine learning models. Feature engineering in the context of e-commerce involves not only cleaning and preprocessing this data but also creating meaningful and predictive features that capture customer behavior, product dynamics, marketing effectiveness, and operational patterns. These features play a critical role in powering recommender systems, conversion prediction models, fraud detection tools, dynamic pricing engines, and customer segmentation solutions.

One of the most fundamental aspects of feature engineering in e-commerce is understanding user behavior. Every click, scroll, or search query is a potential indicator of user intent. By aggregating and transforming raw clickstream data, meaningful behavioral features can be extracted. For example, the number of page views in a session, the time spent on a product detail page, the number of product comparisons, and the frequency of return visits all provide insight into where a customer is in the purchase funnel. Time-based features such as time since last visit, session duration, or time of day of interaction can also help determine a user's level of engagement or readiness to convert. These behavioral indicators often form the basis of conversion rate optimization and personalized recommendation systems.

Product-related features are equally important in shaping e-commerce predictions. These features typically come from structured product catalogs that include attributes such as category, brand, price, availability, ratings, and reviews. Text descriptions, technical specifications, and customer feedback can also be transformed into numerical or categorical features using natural language processing techniques like TF-IDF, sentiment analysis, or topic modeling. Popularity metrics, such as average number of views or purchases per product, as well as inventory-related features like stock level and sell-through rate, provide dynamic signals that change with market trends. Price elasticity features can also be engineered to understand how pricing changes affect sales volumes, which is particularly valuable for dynamic pricing algorithms.

Customer profiles offer another dimension for feature engineering in e-commerce. Historical transaction data allows the creation of features that summarize spending habits, frequency of purchases, average order value, and product preferences. Recency, frequency, and monetary value (RFM) metrics are commonly used to segment customers based on their purchasing behavior. Demographic data, if available, adds further layers of segmentation, enabling personalization based on location, age group, or gender. Customer tenure, defined as the duration since the first purchase, can be combined with lifecycle stage features to tailor marketing efforts. Features indicating customer loyalty, such as subscription status or participation in loyalty programs, provide critical context for understanding future purchasing behavior.

Session-based features also play a pivotal role in real-time e-commerce applications. These features capture actions taken within a single browsing session and can be used to model immediate intent. For example, the sequence of viewed categories, the number of items added to cart, or the frequency of search refinements during a session can signal interest and guide real-time product recommendations. Features such as bounce rate, cart abandonment rate, or session conversion status can be used to predict outcomes of ongoing sessions. Session fingerprinting can also be used to identify recurring users, even in anonymous sessions, based on behavioral patterns.

Marketing and campaign data add another rich source for feature engineering. Click-through rates from ads, email open rates, coupon redemption data, and campaign identifiers help track the effectiveness of marketing strategies. Features can be created to capture the impact of marketing exposure on user behavior, such as the number of ad impressions before conversion, the time between campaign exposure and site visit, or the influence of promotional banners on product views. These features enable models to attribute conversions accurately and to optimize future marketing efforts based on predicted customer responsiveness.

Temporal and event-driven features are particularly relevant in e-commerce, where user activity is often influenced by time-sensitive events. Features indicating whether a transaction took place during a holiday season, end-of-month salary periods, flash sales, or special events like Black Friday can significantly enhance model accuracy. Weekday versus weekend indicators, month-of-year variables, and lag features based on previous periods' sales or visits also help models capture seasonal and cyclical behaviors. These time-based signals are vital for forecasting, inventory planning, and campaign scheduling.

Cross-entity interaction features offer additional modeling power. These are features that capture relationships between different entities, such as users and products, or products and categories. For example, user-product interaction history can be summarized with features like the number of times a specific user viewed a particular product, or how many users who viewed product A also purchased product B. Collaborative filtering techniques can be integrated to build latent features that describe user and item profiles based on interaction matrices. These latent embeddings are then used as input to ranking and recommendation algorithms.

Another critical consideration in e-commerce feature engineering is data freshness. User interests, product availability, and market trends change rapidly. Features need to reflect current realities to remain relevant. This often requires building feature pipelines that automatically update aggregates, calculate rolling statistics, or refresh product scores in near real-time. Using windowed aggregations over recent days or weeks helps models stay attuned to shifting user preferences and purchasing behaviors.

Handling missing or incomplete data is also a common challenge in e-commerce. New users or products may lack historical data, leading to sparsity in features. Imputation strategies, such as using global averages, category-level statistics, or predictive models, help fill these gaps. For completely unseen entities, fallback features based on generalized categories or default embeddings ensure that models can still make reasonable predictions. Feature flags can also be introduced to indicate whether a value was imputed, allowing the model to learn different behaviors for observed and estimated data.

Scalability is essential when dealing with e-commerce data, especially for platforms handling millions of users and products. Feature engineering pipelines must be designed to operate efficiently on distributed systems and be able to compute aggregates across massive datasets quickly. Tools such as feature stores, real-time stream processing, and batch preprocessing frameworks are critical for managing the complexity and volume of data involved in production environments.

Feature engineering in e-commerce is a continuous process that evolves alongside changes in user behavior, product offerings, and technological capabilities. It requires a deep understanding of both the business domain and the technical tools needed to translate raw data into high-quality inputs for machine learning. By focusing on user intent, product context, session dynamics, marketing exposure, and temporal patterns, e-commerce platforms can create features that drive personalization, improve customer satisfaction, and boost business outcomes. These features form the foundation upon which predictive models can operate effectively, making feature engineering not just a technical task but a strategic function at the heart of data-driven commerce.

Handling Imbalanced Data through Feature Design

In many real-world machine learning tasks, especially in domains such as fraud detection, medical diagnosis, rare event prediction, and churn modeling, the dataset is often heavily imbalanced. This means that one class, usually the one of interest, occurs far less frequently than the other. For instance, fraudulent transactions may represent only a small fraction of all financial transactions, yet accurately identifying them is of critical importance. Traditional algorithms can struggle with such imbalances because they tend to be biased toward the majority class, often leading to models that achieve high accuracy while completely ignoring the minority class. One of the most effective and often underutilized strategies to address this problem is through feature design. Carefully crafted features can amplify the signal of minority class examples, making them more distinguishable from the majority class and allowing models to focus better on what matters most.

The core idea behind handling imbalanced data through feature design is to enhance the representation of the minority class by engineering variables that capture specific patterns, behaviors, or attributes associated with it. When the target class is rare, direct learning from the raw features may not be sufficient. Therefore, introducing features that reflect domain-specific anomalies, frequency patterns, or deviation from norms can be particularly beneficial. In the context of fraud detection, for example, simple features like transaction amount or time of transaction might not be very informative on their own, but derived features such as frequency of transactions per hour, sudden changes in spending behavior, or deviation from a user's historical pattern can greatly improve the ability to distinguish fraudulent activity from legitimate behavior.

One powerful technique is the creation of ratio-based features. These features compare values within an instance or across time to highlight deviations. In a credit card transaction dataset, a feature that captures the ratio of the current transaction amount to the average amount over the past week may indicate suspicious activity if the value is unusually high. Similarly, in churn prediction, the ratio of recent engagement to historical engagement can reflect a user's declining interest. Such ratios bring context to raw values, making them more meaningful in distinguishing rare events. When these ratios are engineered using windows of time or specific groups, they further add temporal and relational dimensions to the data that can be critical in detecting anomalies.

Another essential strategy involves capturing rarity and frequency explicitly as features. Count-based features, such as the number of times a user has performed a certain action, the number of purchases of a particular product, or the number of visits to a page, can help differentiate typical behavior from unusual patterns. In imbalanced datasets, the minority class often correlates with unusual or low-frequency behaviors. Encoding these frequencies allows models to learn what constitutes abnormal activity. For categorical features, count encoding or target encoding with smoothing can expose how commonly a category appears and how it relates to the target, thereby giving models a statistical understanding of class distributions.

Time-based features are especially useful in imbalanced settings, where timing or sequence of events can signal rare outcomes. Time since last interaction, duration between specific events, or recency of engagement can reveal latent patterns not captured by static features. For example, in healthcare, the time since the last medical visit, sudden gaps in prescription refills, or compressed sequences of procedures might all suggest underlying risk. When rare outcomes unfold gradually over time, temporal features become critical indicators. Designing these features requires not only understanding the data schema but also the real-world processes behind the recorded events.

Aggregations across groups or entities can also reveal important trends. Calculating statistics such as mean, median, standard deviation, or count at the user, product, or region level helps uncover contextual insights. In cases of imbalance, the minority class may diverge significantly from these aggregate norms. A single instance that deviates from its peer group may be a potential signal. For example, a single user making unusually high-value purchases in a region where most transactions are low-value may indicate fraudulent behavior. Such group-based comparisons are often overlooked but are highly valuable in imbalanced scenarios.

Behavioral features that capture change, variation, or inconsistency over time or across dimensions are also effective. These include features such as variance in purchase categories, inconsistency in login locations, or fluctuation in ratings given by a user. Rare outcomes are frequently associated with unstable or unexpected behavior. By quantifying volatility and change, such features provide clues that static summaries cannot. In a system where most users behave consistently, identifying irregularity becomes a proxy for anomaly detection, and thus a mechanism to handle imbalance indirectly through design.

Feature interactions offer another layer of enhancement. Interactions between features that seem weak in isolation may become highly informative when combined. For example, the combination of a low account balance with a high number of recent withdrawals might signal account compromise. Creating polynomial or multiplicative interactions between features allows the model to capture such complex relationships. These interactions, when informed by domain knowledge, can directly model the conditions that lead to rare outcomes and improve sensitivity to minority class signals.

Another important aspect of feature design in imbalanced data is the use of anomaly scores or unsupervised pretraining. Features that represent the output of an unsupervised model, such as reconstruction error from an autoencoder, cluster membership from a clustering algorithm, or distance from nearest neighbors, can be used as meta-features. These representations often capture the unusualness or distinctiveness of a data point without relying on class labels. In heavily imbalanced datasets, where labeled examples of the minority class are scarce, such unsupervised-derived features can help the model focus on observations that are inherently different from the norm.

Noise handling and feature stability are critical considerations in this context. The presence of noise or mislabeled data can disproportionately affect minority class detection due to its limited representation. Feature engineering should include mechanisms to enhance robustness, such as using median instead of mean for aggregation, using log transformations to reduce skew, or normalizing features within groups to reduce variance. Ensuring that features are stable across training and test datasets helps prevent shifts that degrade model performance when encountering rare examples in production.

Ultimately, handling imbalanced data through feature design is about creating features that provide contrast, context, and clarity. By designing features that highlight the conditions under which the minority class behaves differently from the majority, data scientists can improve the signal-to-noise ratio and enable models to learn effectively despite the imbalance. This process requires a mix of creativity, domain knowledge, statistical insight, and technical skill. It transforms the challenge of imbalance from a limitation into an opportunity, where the thoughtful construction of features becomes the key to unlocking predictive power in the most challenging and impactful machine learning problems.

Feature Engineering for Recommender Systems

Feature engineering plays a central role in the effectiveness of recommender systems, influencing how well algorithms can learn user preferences and item characteristics. It involves the process of selecting, transforming, and creating variables from raw data to improve the performance of a machine learning model. In the context of recommender systems, feature engineering must address both the unique nature of user-item interactions and the challenges posed by sparse, implicit, or noisy data. At its core, the goal is to extract meaningful signals that capture user behavior, item properties, and the context in which interactions occur. The richer and more relevant the features, the more accurate and personalized the recommendations can be.

Recommender systems typically rely on a combination of user data, item metadata, and historical interaction logs. User data might include demographic information, geographic location, and activity patterns, while item metadata may consist of product descriptions, categories, prices, or textual reviews. Historical interactions such as clicks, views, purchases, and ratings reveal latent preferences and are often the most critical component for collaborative filtering-based approaches. However, raw data in its original form rarely contains all the necessary structure for effective modeling. Feature engineering bridges this gap by converting these raw inputs into a format that algorithms can understand and learn from. It allows systems to generalize better, avoid overfitting, and uncover hidden relationships that drive engagement.

One of the primary aspects of feature engineering is dealing with categorical variables. User IDs and item IDs are typical examples, and while they are useful identifiers, on their own they carry no semantic information. A common technique is to encode these IDs using embeddings, which transform them into dense vectors learned through models such as matrix factorization or deep neural networks. These embeddings allow the system to capture latent dimensions of similarity between users and items. Beyond embeddings, categorical features such as user age group, item category, or device type are often one-hot encoded or target encoded depending on the algorithm used. These transformations allow the model to learn associations that would be impossible to detect using raw categorical labels.

Temporal information is another crucial source of insight for feature engineering. The timing of user interactions can reveal seasonal trends, daily habits, or recency effects that significantly impact recommendation relevance. For instance, a user might exhibit different preferences on weekends compared to weekdays or during holidays versus regular workweeks. By extracting features such as time since last interaction, hour of day, day of week, or even time since item release, engineers can help models recognize temporal patterns that enhance predictive accuracy. In time-aware recommender systems, such temporal features are often pivotal in capturing the evolving nature of user interests.

User behavior sequences also provide a rich ground for engineered features. Instead of treating each interaction independently, models can benefit from analyzing the sequence of user actions to understand the context in which preferences emerge. Session-based recommenders often depend heavily on sequence modeling, using recurrent or attention-based architectures that require a meaningful representation of past events. Features like the number of previous clicks, time between interactions, or similarity between consecutive items in a session help characterize the user's intent and state of mind. In these cases, feature engineering involves crafting summary statistics, constructing behavioral profiles, and selecting relevant past interactions to serve as context for predictions.

When working with implicit feedback, such as clicks, views, or dwell time, feature engineering becomes even more important. These signals are often noisy and ambiguous, but they contain valuable information if interpreted correctly. For example, a long dwell time might indicate strong interest, while a short one could suggest dissatisfaction. By combining multiple implicit signals into composite features or applying transformations such as normalization and binning, engineers can clarify ambiguous data and extract more informative patterns. These transformed features help mitigate the challenges of noisy implicit data and support more reliable inferences about user preferences.

Item content is another rich source of engineered features, especially for cold start scenarios where historical interaction data is limited. Natural language processing techniques are frequently employed to extract features from item descriptions, user reviews, or product titles. Text-based features such as TF-IDF vectors, sentiment scores, topic models, or pretrained embeddings can encapsulate the semantic content of an item, allowing the recommender to generalize better to unseen items. In multimedia domains, features derived from images, audio, or video are also essential, requiring the use of convolutional or recurrent neural networks to process raw signals into compact representations that models can use for similarity estimation or clustering.

Cross features are particularly useful when trying to capture interactions between different variables. For instance, a model might benefit from knowing not just that a user is in a certain age group or that an item is of a certain category, but that a user in that age group tends to prefer items of that category. Creating such cross features involves combining two or more variables to model their joint effect. While this increases feature dimensionality, it can significantly boost the model's expressiveness. Careful selection and regularization are required to prevent overfitting and maintain computational efficiency when working with high-dimensional cross features.

Contextual data further enhances the feature space by incorporating situational factors into the recommendation process. These might include device type, browsing environment, user mood inferred from sentiment, or even external factors like weather or local events. Contextual features help recommender systems adapt to the specific conditions under which an interaction occurs, providing a more personalized experience. For example, a user may prefer different types of content when accessing the system from a mobile phone compared to a desktop computer. Feature engineering allows this type of context to influence recommendations in a structured and systematic way.

Feature selection is also a vital part of the process. Not all engineered features contribute positively to the model's performance, and some may introduce noise or redundancy. Techniques such as mutual information, correlation analysis, or model-based importance metrics help identify which features are most predictive. Dimensionality reduction methods like PCA or autoencoders can also be used to compress feature spaces while preserving essential structure. A well-curated feature set not only improves model accuracy but also reduces computational cost and latency, which is critical in real-time recommendation scenarios.

Ultimately, feature engineering for recommender systems is as much an art as it is a science. It requires domain knowledge, creativity, and an understanding of the underlying data-generating process. Whether building a collaborative filtering model, a content-based recommender, or a hybrid system, the careful crafting of features can make the difference between a mediocre system and one that provides truly relevant and satisfying recommendations. The success of modern recommenders often hinges on the richness and relevance of the engineered features, and investing in this stage of development remains one of the most effective ways to boost system performance.

Engineering Features for Fraud Detection

Engineering features for fraud detection is one of the most critical steps in building robust systems capable of identifying suspicious activities with high accuracy. Fraud is inherently deceptive, often hidden beneath layers of legitimate behavior, and its patterns evolve rapidly as fraudsters adapt to detection mechanisms. In such a dynamic environment, raw data alone is rarely sufficient for training models that can effectively distinguish between normal and fraudulent behavior. The transformation of raw transactional, behavioral, and contextual data into engineered features is essential for exposing the subtle signals that suggest anomalies or deceitful patterns. These features serve as the bridge between messy real-world data and the mathematical structures that machine learning algorithms rely on to draw inferences and make predictions.

Fraud detection typically deals with highly imbalanced datasets, where fraudulent cases represent a tiny fraction of the total transactions. This imbalance makes the identification of relevant features even more important, as most machine learning models are biased toward the majority class. Feature engineering can help mitigate this problem by amplifying the signal present in minority class instances, allowing the model to learn what differentiates fraudulent from legitimate actions. For instance, in financial fraud, transactional features such as the amount, frequency, and timing of payments are often more informative when viewed in the context of a user's historical behavior. A single transaction may not raise suspicion, but when compared to the user's typical activity, it could stand out as highly anomalous.

Temporal features are particularly powerful in fraud detection. Fraudsters often exploit time-related vulnerabilities, such as performing multiple rapid transactions before being noticed or conducting high-value actions during off-hours when monitoring may be weaker. By deriving features such as time since the last transaction, average transaction intervals, or transactions occurring at unusual times of day, engineers can highlight temporal inconsistencies that are characteristic of fraud. Additionally, sudden spikes or drops in behavior, such as a user who suddenly starts transferring large sums after months of inactivity, can serve as red flags. Such temporal dynamics are not visible in raw data and require thoughtful aggregation and comparison to reveal their significance.

Location-based features are also crucial, especially in digital platforms where geographic consistency is expected. For example, if a user accesses an account from one country and then, within minutes, performs a transaction from a distant location, this may indicate account compromise. Calculating geographic distances between consecutive logins, measuring IP address entropy, or tracking the number of distinct locations used within a time window can all help surface geographically implausible behavior. These features add a spatial dimension to the analysis, allowing the model to reason about user patterns in both time and space.

Behavioral profiling plays a central role in feature engineering for fraud detection. Rather than relying solely on absolute values, systems benefit from understanding deviations from an established norm. For instance, creating features that compare current behavior to rolling averages or medians enables the system to detect significant shifts. A user consistently making small online purchases who suddenly initiates a high-value international wire transfer may be exhibiting behavior that warrants attention. Feature engineering in this case involves computing user-specific baselines and measuring deviations in real time. These personalized metrics help isolate anomalies that would otherwise be invisible in a general population-level analysis.

One of the most effective strategies in fraud detection is the construction of aggregated features. These features summarize user activity over various time windows, such as total transaction amounts in the past hour, number of login attempts in the past day, or average number of sessions per week. Aggregation allows models to understand frequency, intensity, and recency — all of which are essential in detecting fraudulent intent. Aggregated features often need to be created at multiple granularities to capture both short-term bursts and long-term patterns. Combining these multi-scale summaries helps models understand behavior in context, making it easier to identify unusual activity.

Another essential area of feature engineering is the use of relational data, especially in environments where fraud is committed through collusion. Graph-based features, which represent relationships between users, devices, or accounts, can be extremely informative. For instance, two users making similar transactions from the same IP address, or multiple accounts receiving payments from a common sender, might suggest coordinated behavior. By constructing features such as the number of shared connections, clustering coefficients, or path lengths between entities, engineers can give models insight into the structural relationships that underpin fraud networks. These graph-based representations allow the detection of fraud rings and other organized activities that would be missed by traditional, flat features.

Device fingerprinting provides another rich source of features. Modern fraudsters often use emulators, VPNs, or device spoofing to mask their identity. By extracting and engineering features from device metadata — such as operating system consistency, browser type, screen resolution, or usage patterns — systems can flag devices that show abnormal characteristics or switch identities too frequently. Features that track the entropy or stability of device configurations over time can help identify synthetic behavior or replay attacks, enhancing the system's capacity to filter out malicious devices.

Transaction metadata also offers many opportunities for feature creation. Fields such as merchant category codes, payment channels, transaction descriptions, or currency types can be transformed into categorical features that are either encoded directly or used to compute frequency-based metrics. For instance, a user transacting with a new or rarely used merchant category might be engaging in abnormal behavior. Similarly, identifying mismatches between payment channel and expected activity — such as online transactions using methods typically reserved for in-person use — can raise suspicions. By carefully selecting and encoding these metadata elements, engineers can equip the model with nuanced insights that improve its discriminatory power.

Finally, unsupervised feature generation techniques such as clustering, dimensionality reduction, or autoencoding can be used to derive latent features that capture complex patterns not easily defined through manual engineering. These methods are particularly useful when dealing with high-dimensional behavioral data or when exploring unknown fraud strategies. For example, clustering user activity into behavioral segments can allow the system to detect outliers relative to a user's cluster, rather than to the entire dataset. Autoencoders can compress behavioral data into embeddings that reflect underlying structures, which can then be used as inputs to fraud classifiers.

Feature engineering for fraud detection demands a deep understanding of domain-specific behavior, an awareness of evolving threat landscapes, and the creativity to craft representations that illuminate hidden risk signals. It is a continuous process that must adapt alongside changing user habits and attacker tactics. The features that drive today's models may become obsolete tomorrow, making iterative experimentation and monitoring essential. By carefully crafting features that reflect time, space, behavior, relationships, and metadata, engineers can build systems capable of identifying even the most sophisticated fraud with speed and precision.

Feature Engineering for Medical and Genomic Data

Feature engineering for medical and genomic data presents a uniquely complex challenge that combines the intricacies of biological systems with the rigidity of structured data analysis. The domain encompasses diverse data types such as electronic health records, imaging scans, genetic sequences, clinical notes, laboratory results, and population health statistics. Each of these data sources varies in format, resolution, and reliability, requiring thoughtful preprocessing and transformation to make them usable for predictive modeling. Effective feature engineering in this field is not only essential for model accuracy but also for ensuring that the resulting insights are biologically and clinically meaningful. Unlike traditional domains, the stakes are higher in healthcare and genomics, where the outcome of a model's decision might influence critical medical interventions or reveal genetic susceptibilities.

One of the foundational elements of feature engineering in medical data is dealing with missing and noisy information. Patient records are often incomplete, with vital signs or laboratory values recorded at irregular intervals or entirely absent. Rather than discarding these cases, feature engineering must account for the missingness itself, which can be informative. For example, the absence of a lab test might reflect clinical judgment that the test was unnecessary, suggesting the patient is low-risk. Engineers often create binary indicators for missing values or impute them using methods that respect the time-series nature of medical data, such as forward filling or modeling with temporal decay. This handling of missingness ensures that models capture the implicit reasoning of healthcare providers, rather than being misled by data sparsity.

Temporal relationships within medical data are particularly rich sources of engineered features. Patient health is dynamic, and disease progression often follows distinct patterns over time. Capturing trends in biomarkers, fluctuations in vital signs, or time elapsed between diagnoses provides powerful signals. For instance, a rising trend in creatinine levels might indicate deteriorating kidney function even if individual values fall within normal ranges. Feature engineering in this context involves calculating slopes, variances, lag features, and time gaps between events to describe how a patient's condition evolves. These features must be carefully aligned with clinical relevance to avoid introducing noise, as not all fluctuations carry equal weight in diagnosis or prognosis.

In genomic data, the engineering of features requires a different approach. Raw genetic sequences are often represented as long strings of nucleotide bases or encoded variants across thousands of genomic loci. These sequences must be converted into a structured format that models can learn from. One strategy is to extract known single nucleotide polymorphisms and represent them as binary or categorical features indicating the presence or absence of specific alleles. Another method involves aggregating genetic information into pathways or gene sets, creating features that summarize biological functions or interactions. This biologically-informed reduction of dimensionality helps mitigate the curse of high-dimensional data and emphasizes features with potential causal relationships to disease.

Omics data, such as transcriptomics, proteomics, and metabolomics, add another layer of complexity. These datasets often contain thousands of measurements per sample, with many variables showing strong intercorrelations. Feature engineering in this context often requires statistical or machine learning-based techniques to select relevant signals while reducing noise. Principal component analysis, feature selection based on variance or significance, and autoencoder-derived embeddings are commonly employed to condense information into lower-dimensional representations. At the same time, domain knowledge guides the selection of features tied to known biological mechanisms, helping ensure that models do not merely fit noise but identify pathways with real clinical significance.

Unstructured data sources such as clinical notes and radiology reports offer additional opportunities for feature extraction. Natural language processing techniques can be used to transform free-text into structured indicators of symptoms, diagnoses, medications, or physician sentiment. Named entity recognition, negation detection, and contextual embeddings can all be used to engineer features from clinical narratives that otherwise remain invisible to standard analytical models. These textual features, when combined with structured data, provide a more holistic view of a patient's condition, incorporating subtleties that are often missed by laboratory values or billing codes alone.

Medical imaging data, such as X-rays, MRIs, and CT scans, require feature engineering techniques rooted in computer vision. Traditionally, this involved manual extraction of radiomic features like shape, texture, intensity, or spatial relationships between anatomical structures. With the advent of deep learning, features are increasingly derived from pretrained convolutional neural networks that output compact, abstract representations of image content. However, even with deep learning, feature engineering remains critical. Image-derived features must often be fused with patient metadata or lab values to create multimodal models. The engineering of fusion points, normalization across modalities, and handling of different temporal resolutions are all important steps that affect model performance and interpretability.

Categorical features in medical data, such as diagnosis codes, procedure types, or medication classes, also require careful treatment. These variables often follow hierarchical structures defined by medical taxonomies like ICD codes or ATC classifications. Engineering features that reflect these hierarchies—such as grouping similar conditions or capturing parent-child relationships—enables models to generalize better and avoid overfitting to rare categories. Frequency encoding, embedding layers, and graph-based encodings can all be used to represent complex categorical structures in a model-friendly way, enhancing both performance and clinical alignment.

Patient heterogeneity is another important consideration in this domain. Not all patients respond similarly to disease or treatment, and engineered features must be able to reflect this variability. Segmenting patients into subgroups based on phenotypic similarity or clustering individuals with similar trajectories can help tailor predictions to specific populations. Features that encode comorbidity profiles, polypharmacy patterns, or socioeconomic status provide additional context that enriches predictions and aligns with the real-world complexity of medical decision-making. Such features often require merging data from disparate sources and reconciling inconsistencies, making the engineering process both technical and conceptual.

Finally, feature stability and reproducibility are critical in healthcare settings. Medical models must remain robust across different institutions, populations, and data collection methods. This places a premium on engineered features that are not only predictive but also consistent and interpretable. Engineers must consider how their features will behave under distribution shifts or be understood by clinicians making real-time decisions. Transparency in the feature construction process, adherence to clinical guidelines, and involvement of medical experts throughout the design cycle help ensure that engineered features serve both the model and the people who depend on its outcomes.

Feature engineering for medical and genomic data is therefore not just a technical task, but a multidisciplinary effort that merges data science, clinical expertise, and biological understanding. It requires thoughtful transformation of raw inputs into features that reveal patterns of disease, support early detection, and enable precision medicine. With the right features, models can unlock deep insights into human health, offering tools that extend beyond prediction into explanation, discovery, and intervention.

Model Tuning Fundamentals

Model tuning is a foundational component in the process of building high-performance machine learning systems. While selecting the right algorithm is important, it is rarely sufficient on its own to ensure optimal results. Models are influenced significantly by their hyperparameters—those adjustable settings that govern the learning process, architecture, regularization techniques, and other model-specific behaviors. Hyperparameter tuning, therefore, involves identifying the best combination of these settings to enhance performance, generalization, and stability. The tuning process is both art and science, requiring a deep understanding of how different parameters interact with the data, the model architecture, and each other. It is through careful tuning that a model evolves from a basic prototype into a production-ready solution capable of delivering reliable predictions in a wide range of scenarios.

Hyperparameters differ from trainable parameters in that they are set before the training process begins. For instance, in a decision tree model, the maximum depth or the minimum number of samples required to split a node are examples of hyperparameters. In neural networks, the learning rate, batch size, number of layers, and activation functions play a similar role. These values influence how the model learns from data, how quickly it converges, and how well it generalizes beyond the training set. Choosing poor hyperparameters can lead to underfitting, where the model is too simple to capture the data's complexity, or overfitting, where it becomes too tailored to the training set and performs poorly on unseen data. Therefore, tuning must strike a balance between bias and variance, ensuring that the model neither oversimplifies the problem nor memorizes the training examples.

The first step in tuning is defining an objective function, typically a performance metric that reflects the model's purpose. In classification problems, this might be accuracy, F_1 score, precision, or AUC, depending on the balance between false positives and false negatives the application can tolerate. In regression, mean squared error or mean absolute error are common choices. Once the target metric is selected, the tuning process becomes a search for the hyperparameter values that maximize or minimize this metric, depending on its formulation. It is important to perform tuning using a validation set that is separate from both the training and test datasets. This ensures that the tuning process does not leak information from the test set into the model, preserving the integrity of the evaluation.

Several strategies exist for navigating the hyperparameter space. The simplest is manual tuning, where the practitioner adjusts parameters based on intuition, domain knowledge, or trial and error. While this can work for simple models or experienced users, it is often inefficient and may miss optimal configurations. Grid search offers a more systematic approach, where the model is trained and evaluated across all combinations of predefined hyperparameter values. Although exhaustive, grid search becomes computationally expensive as the number of hyperparameters or their possible values increases. It also suffers from the curse of dimensionality, where most of the computational effort may be spent evaluating suboptimal regions of the search space.

Random search improves on this by selecting random combinations of hyperparameter values within specified ranges. Research has shown that random search is often more efficient than grid search, especially when only a few hyperparameters significantly influence performance. It allows the tuning process to explore a wider variety of combinations and often leads to better results in less time. However, random search still treats all hyperparameter evaluations independently, without learning from previous outcomes. This limitation is addressed by more sophisticated methods such as Bayesian optimization, which models the performance surface and chooses new hyperparameter sets based on previous evaluations, seeking to balance exploration and exploitation.

Bayesian optimization relies on surrogate models, such as Gaussian processes, to predict the likely performance of untested hyperparameter combinations. It chooses the next point to evaluate by optimizing an acquisition function, which quantifies the expected improvement. This method is especially useful when training models is expensive, as it typically converges to a good solution in fewer iterations. Another popular method is Hyperband, which integrates random search with early stopping, allowing the system to allocate resources dynamically and discard poorly performing configurations early in the process. These advanced approaches make model tuning more efficient, scalable, and practical for real-world applications.

Regularization plays a crucial role in the tuning process, as it directly influences the model's ability to generalize. Hyperparameters such as L1 and L2 penalties, dropout rates in neural networks, or the minimum impurity decrease in decision trees are forms of regularization. Tuning these values helps control complexity and prevent the model from fitting noise in the data. Similarly, optimization-related parameters such as learning rate and momentum in gradient descent algorithms must be carefully calibrated. A learning rate that is too high can cause the model to diverge, while one that is too low may result in slow convergence and suboptimal performance. Adaptive learning rate techniques like Adam or RMSprop have hyperparameters of their own that also require tuning, especially in deep learning contexts.

Another critical element is the tuning of model architecture. In deep learning, the number of layers, units per layer, types of activation functions, and layer connectivity all represent design decisions that can be considered hyperparameters. These structural choices determine the model's capacity and inductive biases. Overly complex architectures may fit the training data well but struggle with generalization, while too simple architectures may fail to capture important patterns. Neural architecture search automates this process, using techniques like reinforcement learning or evolutionary algorithms to discover optimal designs. However, this process is often computationally intensive and requires a substantial infrastructure.

During the tuning process, it is also important to monitor model stability and variance across runs. Many models exhibit stochastic behavior due to random initializations, data shuffling, or parallel computations. For this reason, each hyperparameter configuration should be evaluated multiple times, and the average performance should be used as the basis for comparison. Cross-validation is a powerful method for estimating true model performance and helps mitigate the risk of overfitting to a single validation set. Stratified sampling, repeated cross-validation, or nested cross-validation further enhance the robustness of the tuning process and provide better estimates of generalization error.

Model tuning is iterative by nature. Even after identifying a good configuration, changes in data distribution, feature set, or application goals may require retuning. Therefore, it is essential to document the tuning process, track the hyperparameter combinations tested, and store performance metrics in a reproducible and transparent way. Tools and frameworks such as Optuna, Ray Tune, or MLflow facilitate this workflow by automating tuning, logging experiments, and integrating with cloud-based training pipelines. Ultimately, tuning is not just about finding the best numbers, but about refining the model into a trustworthy and high-performing system aligned with the needs of the application.

Hyperparameter Tuning with Grid Search

Hyperparameter tuning with grid search is one of the most widely used methods for improving the performance of machine learning models. While model selection determines the framework or architecture for learning from data, it is hyperparameter tuning that fine-tunes this model to maximize its effectiveness. Grid search offers a systematic and exhaustive approach to this tuning process by evaluating the performance of a model for every possible combination of hyperparameters within a predefined set. This method is particularly appealing for its simplicity, reproducibility, and ability to uncover combinations that may not be obvious through intuition or trial and error. Despite being computationally expensive, grid search remains a go-to method in many practical applications due to its straightforward implementation and interpretability.

In the context of machine learning, hyperparameters refer to the settings or configurations external to the model itself that govern how learning takes place. Unlike model parameters, which are learned from data during training, hyperparameters must be set before the training begins. They include choices such as the learning rate, number of decision tree splits, regularization penalties, kernel functions, or the number of neighbors in a K-nearest neighbors classifier. Each machine learning algorithm has its own set of hyperparameters, and their values can significantly impact the model's ability to learn patterns and generalize to unseen data. Grid search addresses the challenge of finding optimal hyperparameters by performing an exhaustive search over a specified parameter grid.

To perform a grid search, one must first define the hyperparameters to tune and specify a finite list of values for each one. For example, a support vector machine might be tuned using different values of the regularization parameter C and the kernel coefficient gamma. Grid search will then train a model for every combination of these values and evaluate it using a selected performance metric. The combination that yields the best performance on a validation set is selected as the optimal configuration. This exhaustive nature ensures that every possible scenario within the specified grid is considered, offering a comprehensive view of the hyperparameter landscape.

One of the strengths of grid search is its transparency. Because it evaluates all possible combinations in the grid, it is easy to understand and analyze which hyperparameters had the most influence on model performance. This can provide valuable insight into the behavior of the model and guide future refinements. Furthermore, the deterministic nature of grid search makes it highly reproducible. Given the same data and grid definition, it will always produce the same result. This is particularly important in scientific or regulated environments where reproducibility and transparency are essential.

However, the primary drawback of grid search is its computational inefficiency, especially as the number of hyperparameters and candidate values increases. The total number of model evaluations grows exponentially with the number of parameters, making it impractical for large search spaces or when training is computationally expensive. This issue is commonly referred to as the curse of dimensionality. For instance, tuning just five hyperparameters with ten possible values each results in one hundred thousand combinations to evaluate. In such scenarios, grid search can become infeasible unless one has access to substantial computing resources or unless parallel processing is employed to distribute the workload.

Despite this limitation, grid search remains effective in cases where the search space is relatively small or where model training is not prohibitively time-consuming. It is often used in initial experimentation phases to establish baseline performance and to understand how sensitive the model is to changes in different hyperparameters. When used with cross-validation, grid search becomes even more powerful. Cross-validation ensures that the model's performance is not evaluated based on a single arbitrary data split but instead reflects its ability to generalize across multiple subsets of the data. This provides a more reliable estimate of model quality and guards against overfitting to a specific validation set.

To apply grid search efficiently, it is crucial to narrow down the hyperparameter ranges based on prior knowledge, heuristics, or exploratory runs. Including too many irrelevant or extreme values in the grid not only increases computation time but can also dilute the effectiveness of the search. For example, searching over learning rates that are either too small to produce meaningful updates or too large to maintain stable learning can be wasteful. Starting with a coarse grid and then refining the search around the most promising regions is a practical strategy. This approach, sometimes referred to as staged grid search, helps strike a balance between comprehensiveness and efficiency.

Another consideration in grid search is the choice of evaluation metric. The metric should align with the business objective or clinical relevance of the problem. In imbalanced classification problems, for instance, accuracy might be a misleading metric, and alternatives like

F1 score, precision-recall AUC, or Matthews correlation coefficient may be more appropriate. The same grid search process can be applied using any performance measure, but the choice of metric will influence which hyperparameter configuration is selected as optimal. Therefore, defining a meaningful and application-specific metric is a prerequisite for effective tuning.

Implementing grid search is facilitated by many machine learning libraries. In Python, tools such as GridSearchCV in scikit-learn allow users to specify the estimator, parameter grid, scoring metric, and cross-validation strategy in a single function call. These tools handle the complexity of looping over parameter combinations, training models, and collecting performance metrics, providing a convenient and standardized interface. Additionally, the results from a grid search can be analyzed post-hoc to visualize how performance changes across hyperparameter values, helping practitioners gain intuition and guide further exploration.

In some cases, grid search is used not just for tuning model parameters but also for optimizing data preprocessing steps. For example, parameters for normalization, feature selection thresholds, or dimensionality reduction components can be included in the grid. This allows for a holistic approach to tuning the entire machine learning pipeline, from raw data to final predictions. By integrating preprocessing and model tuning into the same search space, practitioners ensure that interactions between different stages are considered, which can result in more robust and well-performing models.

Hyperparameter tuning with grid search remains a cornerstone technique in the data scientist's toolkit. Its strength lies in its clarity and exhaustive coverage, making it ideal for smaller search spaces and scenarios where interpretability and reproducibility are paramount. While more sophisticated optimization techniques exist for high-dimensional or computationally intensive problems, the foundational principles of grid search continue to play a critical role in developing well-tuned, reliable, and high-performing machine learning models.

Random Search for Hyperparameter Optimization

Random search for hyperparameter optimization offers a compelling alternative to grid search by addressing its inefficiencies and limitations, particularly in high-dimensional spaces. While grid search systematically explores all possible combinations within a defined hyperparameter grid, random search samples combinations at random from specified distributions or value ranges. This randomness introduces greater flexibility and often leads to better results in less time, especially when only a few hyperparameters have a significant influence on model performance. In practice, random search is widely used because it balances computational efficiency with the ability to explore a diverse range of hyperparameter settings, making it suitable for both quick experiments and large-scale production models.

Hyperparameters govern the behavior of machine learning algorithms but are not learned from the training data. These parameters, such as the learning rate in gradient descent, the number of estimators in ensemble methods, the depth of decision trees, or the dropout rate in neural networks, must be set prior to training. Because the number of possible combinations can be vast, especially when multiple hyperparameters are involved, it becomes impractical to evaluate them all exhaustively. Grid search attempts to do exactly that, but in doing so, it wastes significant computational resources exploring combinations that contribute little to model performance. Random search counters this by treating the search space as a probabilistic domain, where parameter combinations are drawn from user-defined distributions.

The theoretical advantage of random search lies in the observation that, in many models, not all hyperparameters are equally important. A small subset of hyperparameters often has a large effect on performance, while others exert minimal influence. Grid search allocates equal resources to every parameter in the grid, which means it may spend much of its time evaluating unimportant settings. Random search, by contrast, has a higher chance of sampling values from the influential dimensions more frequently, simply because it is not constrained to a fixed grid. This randomness makes it more likely to stumble upon optimal or near-optimal configurations early in the process, leading to faster convergence and better outcomes with fewer iterations.

To conduct a random search, practitioners define a search space for each hyperparameter. This can include discrete sets of values, continuous ranges, or probability distributions. For example, a learning rate might be sampled from a log-uniform distribution between 0.0001 and 0.1, reflecting the fact that orders of magnitude often matter more than small linear increments. The number of units in a neural network layer might be drawn from an integer range between 32 and 512. The model is then trained and evaluated using a fixed number of randomly sampled combinations. These evaluations are typically done using cross-validation or a held-out validation set to ensure reliable performance estimates. The best-performing configuration according to the chosen metric is selected at the end of the process.

Random search provides an excellent foundation for iterative experimentation. Since each iteration is independent, it allows easy parallelization across multiple processors or machines. This enables faster exploration of the hyperparameter space and makes random search highly scalable. Furthermore, unlike grid search, random search does not suffer from the curse of dimensionality to the same extent. As the number of hyperparameters increases, grid search becomes exponentially more expensive, while random search simply continues sampling regardless of dimensionality. This makes it especially valuable in deep learning, where models may have dozens of tunable parameters and where exhaustive search is often computationally prohibitive.

Another benefit of random search is its adaptability. Practitioners can modify the sampling strategy based on prior knowledge, adjusting the distributions or ranges to focus on promising regions of the hyperparameter space. For example, if previous experiments indicate that the learning rate performs best around 0.01, the search can be biased toward that region by narrowing the distribution or shifting its mean. This flexibility allows random search to incorporate empirical knowledge without hardcoding rigid combinations. It can also be used in a multi-phase strategy, where an initial broad search is followed by a more focused search around the best values discovered. This staged approach further enhances efficiency and performance.

In practical applications, random search is often implemented using tools such as scikit-learn's RandomizedSearchCV, Keras Tuner, or more general-purpose libraries like Ray Tune or Optuna. These tools support specification of parameter distributions, parallel execution, and integration with cross-validation schemes. They also provide logging and tracking capabilities, which are essential for comparing different runs and identifying trends. Users can define the number of iterations or time budget for the search, enabling them to control resource consumption and stop the process when diminishing returns are observed. Because random search is inherently stochastic, repeating the process with different random seeds can also yield additional insights and improve robustness.

Random search is not without its challenges. Since the method relies on random sampling, it offers no guarantees of finding the global optimum, and it may occasionally miss important regions of the search space if the number of iterations is too low. However, these limitations are generally outweighed by its speed, simplicity, and ability to uncover effective configurations quickly. To mitigate the risk of poor coverage, practitioners often increase the number of iterations, adjust the distributions, or run multiple random searches with different seeds. Additionally, combining random search with early stopping criteria can further improve efficiency by terminating poor-performing models before training completes, allowing resources to be reallocated to more promising configurations.

The effectiveness of random search also depends on the design of the hyperparameter space. Selecting appropriate ranges and distributions is crucial for successful optimization. Uniform distributions are suitable when all values are equally likely, while log-uniform distributions are more appropriate when dealing with parameters that span several orders of magnitude. Categorical hyperparameters, such as activation functions or kernel types, can be included in the random search by assigning them as discrete choices. The thoughtful construction of the search space can dramatically influence the quality of the results, and this step often benefits from domain knowledge or preliminary experimentation.

In many real-world machine learning workflows, random search serves as a first-line method for hyperparameter tuning. Its ease of implementation, ability to handle arbitrary parameter types, and compatibility with parallel computing environments make it a practical choice in a wide variety of settings. Whether optimizing a simple logistic regression model or a deep convolutional neural network, random search provides a reliable way to explore the hyperparameter landscape without the exhaustive demands of grid search. It introduces an element of unpredictability that, paradoxically, often leads to more consistent and superior outcomes when compared to more rigid strategies. By embracing randomness, practitioners gain a powerful tool for navigating complex optimization problems and achieving high-performing models in less time.

Bayesian Optimization for Model Tuning

Bayesian optimization for model tuning represents one of the most sophisticated and effective approaches to finding optimal hyperparameters in machine learning. Unlike grid search or random search, which explore the hyperparameter space blindly or uniformly, Bayesian optimization builds a probabilistic model of the objective function and uses it to make informed decisions about where to sample next. This guided strategy allows it to balance exploration and exploitation, seeking out promising regions of the search space while avoiding unnecessary evaluations in areas that are unlikely to improve performance. The result is a more efficient optimization process, particularly well-suited for scenarios where training models is computationally expensive and the hyperparameter space is complex or high-dimensional.

At the heart of Bayesian optimization is the idea that evaluating a machine learning model is costly. Each training and validation cycle can consume minutes, hours, or even days, depending on the model complexity and dataset size. Therefore, minimizing the number of evaluations while still finding a high-performing configuration is crucial. Bayesian optimization treats the model tuning task as a black-box optimization problem, where the true function mapping hyperparameters to performance is unknown and expensive to evaluate. By building a surrogate model—typically a probabilistic model such as a Gaussian process—the algorithm can estimate this function and make decisions about where to evaluate next based on both expected performance and uncertainty.

The optimization process begins with an initial set of randomly sampled hyperparameter configurations. These samples are evaluated using the machine learning model, and their results are used to fit the surrogate model. The surrogate model serves as an inexpensive approximation of the true objective function, providing both a predicted performance value and a measure of confidence or uncertainty for any given set of hyperparameters. This uncertainty is key to the exploration-exploitation trade-off. Areas with high uncertainty might reveal better performance than currently known, while areas with low uncertainty but high expected performance are worth exploiting. This balance is governed by an acquisition function, a mathematical tool that guides the selection of the next point to evaluate.

Common acquisition functions include expected improvement, probability of improvement, and upper confidence bound. These functions are designed to quantify the utility of evaluating a new hyperparameter configuration. For example, expected improvement estimates how much better the new point is expected to perform compared to the current best. By maximizing the acquisition function, Bayesian optimization selects the most promising next configuration, evaluates it, updates the surrogate model with the new result, and repeats the process. This iterative cycle continues until a stopping criterion is met, such as a fixed number of iterations, a time budget, or lack of sufficient improvement.

One of the key strengths of Bayesian optimization is its sample efficiency. Because it uses information from previous evaluations to inform future ones, it often finds high-performing configurations with far fewer model evaluations than random or grid search. This is especially beneficial in deep learning or ensemble methods, where each model training session can be time-consuming. Additionally, Bayesian optimization can handle noisy objective functions, which is common in machine learning due to factors like data sampling variability or stochastic training procedures. The probabilistic nature of the surrogate model allows it to account for this noise, providing robust estimates and helping the algorithm avoid being misled by outlier results.

Bayesian optimization is also highly flexible. While Gaussian processes are the most commonly used surrogate models, other methods such as random forests, tree-structured Parzen estimators, and Bayesian neural networks have also been successfully applied. This flexibility allows Bayesian optimization to scale to larger datasets and more complex search spaces. Moreover, it can accommodate both continuous and categorical hyperparameters, making it suitable for a wide variety of machine learning tasks. Categorical parameters, such as optimizer type or activation function, are handled through encoding techniques or specialized surrogate models that can deal with discrete spaces.

In practice, implementing Bayesian optimization has been greatly simplified by the availability of modern libraries and tools. Libraries like Optuna, Hyperopt, Spearmint, and BoTorch provide robust frameworks for defining search spaces, configuring surrogate models and acquisition functions, and running optimization loops. These tools integrate easily with popular machine learning frameworks, making it straightforward to apply Bayesian optimization to real-world problems. They often include features such as pruning underperforming trials, asynchronous execution, and automatic logging of experiments, further enhancing usability and efficiency.

Despite its many advantages, Bayesian optimization does come with challenges. The surrogate model must be refitted after each new observation, which can become computationally expensive as the number of samples grows. Gaussian processes in particular scale poorly with the number of observations, typically requiring cubic time complexity in relation to the dataset size. This makes them less suitable for very large tuning runs unless approximations or alternative surrogate models are used. Additionally, Bayesian optimization assumes that the objective function is relatively smooth and that small changes in hyperparameters result in small changes in performance. While this assumption holds in many cases, highly rugged or discontinuous search spaces may cause the surrogate model to struggle, reducing the effectiveness of the optimization process.

Another practical consideration is the initial design phase, during which the algorithm collects its first few observations. These initial samples are usually generated randomly and should be diverse enough to provide the surrogate model with a good representation of the search space. Too few initial points can lead to poor surrogate model performance, while too many can waste valuable evaluation budget. This phase is critical to setting the stage for efficient optimization and is often guided by heuristics or domain knowledge to select meaningful starting configurations.

Bayesian optimization also lends itself well to multi-objective and constrained optimization problems. In many real-world applications, one might want to optimize for accuracy while also minimizing model size or inference time. Extensions of Bayesian optimization can model multiple objectives simultaneously, finding a Pareto frontier of optimal trade-offs. Similarly, constraints such as memory usage or training time can be incorporated into the optimization process, guiding the search toward configurations that meet all requirements. This makes Bayesian optimization a powerful tool not just for pure performance tuning but also for holistic system design in production environments.

As machine learning continues to grow in scale and complexity, the importance of efficient and intelligent hyperparameter optimization strategies becomes ever more apparent. Bayesian optimization offers a principled and effective solution by combining the power of probabilistic modeling with decision theory. It turns the tuning process into a guided exploration of the unknown, continually learning from past results to make smarter choices. This adaptability, combined with its efficiency and robustness, positions Bayesian optimization as a central technique for anyone looking to extract the highest possible performance from their machine learning models with limited computational resources.

Tuning Decision Trees and Random Forests

Tuning decision trees and random forests is a fundamental process in building interpretable, efficient, and accurate models for both classification and regression tasks. These tree-based algorithms are popular because of their flexibility, ability to handle mixed data types, robustness to outliers, and relatively minimal preprocessing requirements. However, their performance is highly dependent on the correct configuration of hyperparameters. If not tuned properly, a decision tree can easily overfit the training data, creating overly complex models that fail to generalize. Likewise, an untuned random forest can become computationally expensive and inefficient, while offering only marginal improvements over a single tree. Hyperparameter tuning allows these models to reach their full potential by balancing complexity, depth, and diversity.

A decision tree is a hierarchical structure where each node splits the data according to a specific feature and threshold. This structure is recursively built by selecting the best possible splits at each step, often using metrics such as Gini impurity or entropy in classification, and mean squared error in regression. One of the most important hyperparameters is the maximum depth of the tree. This determines how far the tree is allowed to grow. A shallow tree may not capture the necessary complexity of the data and lead to underfitting. On the other hand, a very deep tree may memorize the training data, fitting even the noise, which leads to poor generalization on unseen data. Tuning the maximum depth is crucial for finding the right trade-off between bias and variance.

Another critical hyperparameter is the minimum number of samples required to split a node. This value can control how easily the tree continues to grow and how finely it slices the feature space. A small value allows the tree to grow deep and granular, potentially increasing accuracy on the training set at the cost of overfitting. A larger value forces the tree to stop splitting early, leading to simpler and more general models. Similarly, the minimum number of samples required to be at a leaf node plays a similar role, influencing how many examples must be present for a split to be valid. Adjusting these values can regularize the tree and prevent it from becoming too specialized.

The choice of the splitting criterion also plays a role in how the tree behaves. Gini impurity and information gain (based on entropy) often produce similar results, but in some datasets, one may offer a slight advantage. For regression tasks, using mean squared error or mean absolute error affects how the tree optimizes its predictions. While the criterion does not drastically change the structure of the tree, it can influence the selection of features and thresholds, especially in datasets with noisy or skewed distributions.

In the case of random forests, the tuning process becomes more complex because the model is an ensemble of decision trees. Each tree is trained on a random subset of the data with replacement, and at each split, it considers only a random subset of the features. This randomness introduces diversity among the trees, which helps reduce variance and improve generalization. However, it also introduces new hyperparameters that need to be tuned. The number of trees in the forest is a primary factor. A small number of trees may not capture enough diversity and lead to unstable predictions. A larger number of trees generally improves performance, but with diminishing returns and increased computational cost. Identifying the point at which adding more trees no longer yields substantial gains is a key part of tuning.

The maximum number of features considered at each split is another important hyperparameter in random forests. This controls the degree of randomness and decorrelation among the trees. Using all features at every split makes the individual trees more similar to each other, which may reduce the benefit of ensembling. Limiting the number of features allows the trees to explore different structures and reduces correlation, often leading to better ensemble performance. For classification tasks, the square root of the total number of features is a common default, while for regression, using one-third of the features is often effective. However, these defaults may not be optimal for every dataset, and tuning this parameter can have a significant impact.

Bootstrap sampling, which allows trees in the forest to train on random samples with replacement, can also be toggled. While it is typically enabled by default and contributes to variance reduction, disabling it and using the entire dataset for each tree may improve performance in low-variance datasets. In addition to bootstrap, tuning the maximum depth of individual trees within the forest is important. Deep trees can memorize their bootstrapped samples, while shallow trees may not capture enough detail. Finding the right depth ensures that each tree contributes meaningfully to the ensemble without overfitting.

Out-of-bag evaluation is a technique specific to random forests that provides an internal validation mechanism. Since each tree is trained on a bootstrap sample, about one-third of the data is left out and can be used to estimate performance. Tuning based on out-of-bag error can save time by avoiding the need for separate validation sets or cross-validation, although it is less reliable in small datasets. It is especially useful for getting a quick sense of how the model is performing during hyperparameter optimization.

The combination of tree-specific and ensemble-specific hyperparameters makes tuning random forests more nuanced than tuning a single decision tree. It often involves balancing tree depth, split thresholds, and feature randomness to achieve both low bias and low variance. In practice, tuning is done using cross-validation or randomized search, where combinations of hyperparameters are evaluated on holdout sets. Random search can be particularly effective for random forests, as not all hyperparameters contribute equally to performance, and it is more efficient than grid search in high-dimensional spaces.

Feature importance scores, which are a natural byproduct of both decision trees and random forests, can guide the tuning process. By identifying which features contribute most to prediction, it is possible to engineer more effective inputs or prune irrelevant features. These scores also improve model interpretability, making tree-based models attractive in domains where understanding decisions is important. During tuning, observing changes in feature importance across configurations can offer insights into model behavior and stability.

Tuning decision trees and random forests ultimately comes down to understanding the trade-offs imposed by each hyperparameter. Each setting has implications for model complexity, computational cost, and generalization ability. A well-tuned tree captures the essential patterns in the data without overfitting, and a well-tuned forest leverages ensemble diversity to amplify predictive power. When approached systematically, the tuning process can transform these already powerful algorithms into highly effective tools for a wide range of real-world tasks.

Regularization Techniques in Linear Models

Regularization techniques in linear models are fundamental tools used to address the issue of overfitting and to enhance the generalization ability of models when applied to new, unseen data. In the realm of supervised learning, linear regression and logistic regression are among the most interpretable and widely used algorithms, particularly in domains that demand transparency and simplicity. However, these models can suffer from high variance, especially when the number of features is large or when multicollinearity exists among the input variables. Regularization serves as a mechanism to impose constraints on the model's parameters, effectively penalizing complexity and guiding the optimization process toward simpler, more stable solutions.

The core concept of regularization involves augmenting the loss function of a linear model with a penalty term that increases as the magnitude of the model coefficients increases. This penalization discourages the model from assigning excessively large weights to any single feature, which is often a symptom of overfitting. By incorporating such penalties, the model is forced to strike a balance between fitting the training data accurately and maintaining a level of simplicity that promotes better generalization on test data. The most commonly used regularization techniques in linear models are L1 regularization, known as Lasso, and L2 regularization, known as Ridge. Each of these techniques has distinct mathematical properties and practical implications that influence how they behave in different modeling scenarios.

L2 regularization, or Ridge regression, adds the sum of the squares of the coefficients to the loss function. This squared penalty tends to shrink the coefficients toward zero but rarely drives them to exactly zero. The effect of this is a smoothing of the model, where all features contribute to the prediction to some extent, but none dominate excessively. Ridge regression is particularly effective when dealing with multicollinearity, as it stabilizes the estimation process by reducing the variance of the coefficients. The regularization strength is controlled by a hyperparameter, often denoted as alpha or lambda, which determines the trade-off between the original loss and the penalty term. As this parameter increases, the model becomes more constrained, and the coefficients are further shrunk.

In contrast, L1 regularization, or Lasso regression, adds the sum of the absolute values of the coefficients to the loss function. Unlike Ridge, the L1 penalty can drive some coefficients exactly to zero, effectively performing feature selection during the learning process. This sparsity-inducing property makes Lasso especially useful when dealing with high-dimensional datasets where only a small subset of features is expected to be relevant. Lasso encourages simpler models that are easier to interpret and often more robust. However, in cases of highly correlated features, Lasso tends to arbitrarily select one and ignore the others, which may not be ideal if group-wise interpretation is needed.

To address the limitations of both Ridge and Lasso, a hybrid approach known as Elastic Net has been developed. Elastic Net combines both L1 and L2 penalties in a single regularization framework. This technique allows the model to benefit from the feature selection capabilities of Lasso while also maintaining the stability and grouping effect of Ridge. The balance between the L1 and L2 components is governed by an additional hyperparameter that can be tuned to emphasize one penalty over the other. Elastic Net is especially advantageous in situations where there are multiple correlated predictors and a sparse solution is still desired. Its flexibility and effectiveness make it a popular choice in many real-world applications.

Choosing the appropriate regularization technique and tuning its hyperparameters is critical for achieving optimal performance. This process typically involves cross-validation, where the data is split into multiple subsets, and the model is trained and validated across these folds to estimate its generalization error. By systematically varying the regularization strength and evaluating the model's performance, practitioners can identify the configuration that provides the best balance between bias and variance. Regularization not only helps reduce overfitting but also improves numerical stability, especially when the feature matrix is ill-conditioned or nearly singular.

The impact of regularization extends beyond just predictive accuracy. It plays a significant role in model interpretability, especially in fields such as healthcare, finance, and the social sciences, where understanding the influence of each variable is essential. Ridge regression allows all features to remain in the model, which is useful when interpretability requires accounting for all potential influences, even if weak. Lasso, on the other hand, provides a more concise explanation by selecting a small number of impactful features, which can simplify the communication of results and support decision-making processes. Elastic Net, by combining these perspectives, offers a flexible tool that can be tailored to the specific needs of the domain.

Another aspect of regularization is its role in dealing with noisy data. In real-world datasets, noise and measurement errors are often unavoidable. A model trained without regularization may attempt to fit this noise, leading to poor performance on future data. Regularization mitigates this by favoring simpler models that are less sensitive to fluctuations in the training data. In this way, regularization acts as a form of inductive bias, guiding the learning algorithm toward solutions that align with the assumption that simpler models are more likely to generalize well.

Beyond standard regression tasks, regularization techniques are also applied in generalized linear models and other extensions such as logistic regression, Poisson regression, and multinomial classification. In classification problems, the same principles apply: regularization constrains the coefficients to prevent overfitting and ensures that the decision boundary is not overly complex. In logistic regression, for example, the sigmoid function introduces non-linearity, but the linear relationship between the features and the log-odds can still lead to overfitting if not regularized. Applying L_1, L_2, or Elastic Net penalties helps to manage this complexity and produce more reliable classifiers.

Implementing regularization is straightforward in most modern machine learning libraries. Frameworks such as scikit-learn, TensorFlow, and PyTorch provide built-in support for L_1 and L_2 penalties, allowing users to easily integrate regularization into their models. The key challenge lies not in applying the technique, but in understanding its implications, tuning it appropriately, and interpreting the resulting models within the context of the data and the problem domain. Regularization remains one of the most powerful and essential tools for any practitioner working with linear models, offering a principled approach to controlling complexity, improving generalization, and enhancing the stability of predictive systems.

Tuning Gradient Boosted Trees

Tuning gradient boosted trees is a critical step in extracting the maximum predictive power from one of the most effective and widely used machine learning algorithms. Gradient boosting is an ensemble learning method that builds models sequentially, where each new model attempts to correct the errors of the previous ones. It combines multiple weak learners, typically decision trees, into a strong overall predictor. Because of its flexibility and ability to capture complex patterns in data, gradient boosting has become a dominant choice in many structured data problems. However, its performance is highly sensitive to the settings of its numerous hyperparameters. Without careful tuning, a gradient boosted model can suffer from overfitting, underfitting, slow convergence, or unnecessarily long training times.

One of the most important hyperparameters in gradient boosted trees is the learning rate, also known as eta in some implementations. The learning rate determines the contribution of each new tree to the overall ensemble. A smaller learning rate reduces the influence of each tree and allows the model to learn slowly and carefully, often leading to better generalization. However, smaller learning rates typically require more boosting iterations to reach optimal performance. A higher learning rate speeds up the learning process but increases the risk of overfitting. Tuning the learning rate involves finding the right balance between speed and accuracy, often in conjunction with the number of boosting rounds or trees. The most effective strategy is to use a low learning rate with a higher number of trees, allowing the model to refine its predictions gradually.

The number of trees or boosting rounds is directly related to the learning rate and is another key hyperparameter. Too few trees can lead to underfitting, where the model fails to capture the underlying data structure. Too many trees, especially with a high learning rate, can result in overfitting, where the model memorizes the training data and performs poorly on new inputs. Cross-validation is commonly used to determine the optimal number of boosting rounds by monitoring performance on a validation set and stopping early if the performance stops improving. This technique, known as early stopping, is a practical and efficient method for preventing overfitting while minimizing training time.

Tree-specific parameters also play a significant role in the tuning process. The maximum depth of each tree controls the complexity of individual trees in the ensemble. Deeper trees can capture more intricate patterns in the data but are also more prone to overfitting. Shallow trees, on the other hand, promote generalization but may not capture all necessary interactions among features. Tuning the tree depth is essential for managing the bias-variance trade-off in gradient boosting. In many applications, depths between three and eight provide a good balance, although the optimal value depends on the specific dataset and problem.

Closely related to tree depth is the minimum number of samples required to make a split, sometimes referred to as min_child_weight or min_samples_split depending on the implementation. This parameter prevents the model from creating splits that are based on very few data points, which can lead to overly specific rules and reduce the model's generalizability. Increasing this parameter encourages the model to focus on broader patterns and prevents it from overreacting to noise in the data. It acts as a regularization mechanism, helping to constrain the growth of the tree and improve model robustness.

Another crucial parameter is the subsample ratio, which determines the fraction of the training data used to grow each tree. Using a subsample value less than one introduces randomness into the training process, similar to the bagging technique in random forests. This randomness helps reduce overfitting by decorrelating the trees and making the ensemble more robust. Subsampling is especially useful when the model is large or the data is noisy. However, setting the subsample ratio too low can lead to underfitting, as each tree has access to only a small portion of the data. A value between 0.5 and 1.0 is typically effective, with the exact value depending on the size and noise level of the dataset.

The colsample_bytree parameter, or feature subsampling rate, determines the fraction of features to be considered when building each tree. Like subsample, this parameter introduces randomness and helps prevent overfitting. By allowing each tree to see only a subset of the features, the model becomes less reliant on any single input variable and learns to build more generalized rules. Feature subsampling is particularly beneficial in datasets with a large number of features, where some may be irrelevant or redundant. Tuning this parameter involves balancing diversity and accuracy across the trees in the ensemble.

Regularization parameters such as gamma, lambda, and alpha further control the complexity of the model. Gamma defines the minimum loss reduction required to make a split, acting as a threshold that discourages unnecessary complexity. Higher values of gamma make the algorithm more conservative, pruning branches that do not contribute significantly to improving the model's performance. Lambda and alpha represent L2 and L1 regularization on the weights of the leaves, respectively. These penalties help control the magnitude of the leaf values and can improve generalization, especially in datasets with noisy or high-dimensional features. Adjusting these parameters allows the model to be tailored more precisely to the data and the task.

In many practical implementations of gradient boosting, such as XGBoost, LightGBM, or CatBoost, tuning involves not only the core boosting parameters but also choices about how data is handled and processed. For instance, LightGBM uses histogram-based algorithms and leaf-wise growth strategies that can significantly affect performance and memory usage. CatBoost includes built-in support for categorical features and automatic handling of missing values, which can simplify preprocessing but introduces its own tuning challenges. Each library offers unique advantages and requires a slightly different approach to parameter tuning, though the underlying principles remain consistent across implementations.

To effectively tune gradient boosted trees, practitioners often rely on systematic search strategies like grid search, random search, or Bayesian optimization. These methods help navigate the high-dimensional hyperparameter space and identify configurations that lead to optimal performance. Because training gradient boosted models can be computationally intensive, it is important to monitor validation metrics closely and leverage tools like early stopping to avoid unnecessary evaluations. Visualization of learning curves, feature importance, and validation scores over time can also provide valuable insights during the tuning process and help guide adjustments.

Tuning gradient boosted trees is not a one-time task but an iterative process that evolves alongside the model's development. As new features are added, preprocessing steps are changed, or the nature of the data shifts, the optimal hyperparameters may change as well. Maintaining a disciplined and informed tuning process ensures that the model continues to perform at a high level, remains interpretable where needed, and scales effectively with the demands of real-world applications. By understanding the function and interaction of each parameter, practitioners can unlock the full power of gradient boosting and create models that are both accurate and robust across a wide range of predictive tasks.

Hyperparameter Tuning in Neural Networks

Hyperparameter tuning in neural networks is a delicate and essential process that plays a decisive role in the final performance of a deep learning model. Unlike traditional machine learning models, neural networks contain a vast array of hyperparameters, many of which have a strong influence on the training dynamics, model capacity, and ultimately, the quality of predictions. These hyperparameters govern nearly every aspect of the training pipeline, from the structure of the network itself to the optimization algorithm used, learning rate schedules, regularization techniques, batch sizes, and more. Finding the optimal combination is not a trivial task. It requires a deep understanding of how each setting interacts with the others and how the model responds to data of varying complexity, scale, and quality.

One of the most critical hyperparameters in any neural network is the learning rate. This single parameter controls the size of the steps that the optimization algorithm takes while updating weights based on the gradients of the loss function. If the learning rate is too high, the model may diverge, overshooting the optimal minima and leading to unstable training. If it is too low, training becomes slow and may get stuck in local minima or saddle points. Learning rate schedules and adaptive learning methods like Adam, RMSProp, or AdaGrad help mitigate this challenge, but the initial learning rate still needs careful tuning. Often, learning rate is tuned on a logarithmic scale, and practitioners experiment with values that vary by several orders of magnitude to find the optimal range.

The architecture of the neural network introduces several more hyperparameters, each of which significantly impacts model behavior. These include the number of layers, the number of neurons per layer, and the choice of activation functions. The depth of a network defines its capacity to capture complex representations. Shallow networks may not be expressive enough to model high-dimensional data, while deeper networks can overfit, particularly if the data is limited. Width, or the number of units in each layer, determines how much information each layer can hold. Too few units restrict learning capacity, while too many can result in unnecessary computational cost and overfitting. The choice of activation function—such as ReLU, sigmoid, tanh, or newer variants like GELU or Swish—affects the non-linear transformation of data and has implications for gradient propagation. Some functions are better suited for specific tasks or architectures, and selecting the appropriate one is a key part of tuning.

Batch size is another hyperparameter that influences training dynamics. Smaller batch sizes tend to produce noisier gradient estimates, which can help in escaping local minima and improve generalization. Larger batch sizes provide more stable updates and can leverage hardware acceleration more effectively, but they may lead to models that generalize poorly. There is no one-size-fits-all batch size, and its optimal value often depends on the dataset, network architecture, and available computational resources. Often, tuning involves trying different batch sizes in powers of two and observing their effect on convergence speed and validation performance.

Regularization is crucial in preventing neural networks from overfitting to the training data. Techniques like dropout, L1 or L2 regularization, and batch normalization all introduce additional hyperparameters that require careful tuning. Dropout rate, for example, determines the fraction of neurons to randomly deactivate during training. Too high a dropout rate can undercut the network's learning capacity, while too low a rate may provide insufficient regularization. Similarly, the strength of L1 or L2 penalties must be adjusted to balance between encouraging sparsity or smoothness in the weights and preserving the model's ability to learn from complex patterns. Batch normalization includes parameters such as momentum and epsilon, which can affect the stability and speed of training. These regularization techniques, when tuned properly, contribute to better generalization and model robustness.

Another important aspect of tuning involves the optimizer. The optimizer defines how the network updates its weights and biases during training. While stochastic gradient descent is the most basic method, more advanced optimizers like Adam, Nadam, or Adadelta have become common due to their adaptive learning rate capabilities. Each optimizer comes with its own set of hyperparameters, such as momentum, beta coefficients, or epsilon values. Tuning these can have a significant impact on convergence behavior, especially in deeper networks or in models trained on noisy data. Selecting the right optimizer and fine-tuning its parameters often involves a mixture of empirical testing and experience with similar tasks.

In addition to tuning parameters for a single training run, learning rate schedules and early stopping criteria play an integral role in training strategy. Schedulers adjust the learning rate based on training progression, either by reducing it when the validation loss plateaus or by following a predefined decay function. Step decay, exponential decay, and cosine annealing are popular strategies that require their own hyperparameters, such as decay rate and step size. Early stopping, on the other hand, halts training when no improvement in validation loss is seen for a certain number of epochs. This patience value, as well as the minimum delta required for improvement, must be tuned to ensure that the model is neither stopped too early nor allowed to overfit.

The initialization of network weights is another subtle but impactful factor. Although many deep learning frameworks offer default initialization methods, tuning initial weights or choosing initialization schemes like He, Xavier, or LeCun can make a notable difference in how quickly and effectively a model trains. Poor initialization can slow down convergence or cause the gradients to vanish or explode, especially in deep networks. Although not traditionally thought of as tunable hyperparameters, initialization strategies can and should be experimented with when performance issues arise.

The complexity of neural network tuning also invites automated approaches. Tools like Hyperopt, Optuna, Keras Tuner, and Ray Tune allow practitioners to define search spaces and leverage techniques like random search, Bayesian optimization, or genetic algorithms to explore the landscape of hyperparameter configurations efficiently. These methods are particularly useful when dealing with many interacting hyperparameters, where manual tuning becomes impractical. These frameworks also support pruning underperforming trials and using asynchronous evaluations, which further reduce computational overhead and allow for more rapid experimentation.

Hyperparameter tuning in neural networks is both a science and an art. It requires a combination of theoretical understanding, empirical observation, and practical intuition. Each model, dataset, and task introduces its own nuances, and what works well in one context may fail in another. A well-tuned neural network is not simply a function of high-performing defaults but the result of deliberate experimentation, rigorous validation, and iterative refinement. It is through this process that neural networks can be transformed from general-purpose learners into finely crafted models capable of solving complex, real-world problems with precision and reliability.

Dropout, Batch Normalization, and Learning Rate Schedules

Dropout, batch normalization, and learning rate schedules are three powerful techniques that play a critical role in the training and generalization of neural networks. While each addresses different aspects of model performance and training dynamics, together they form a foundation for creating deep learning models that are both robust and efficient. These techniques are not merely auxiliary components but are deeply integrated into modern training pipelines, often making the difference between a poorly performing model and one that achieves state-of-the-art results. Understanding their mechanics, effects, and how to tune them effectively is essential for any practitioner working with neural networks, regardless of the task or domain.

Dropout is a regularization method designed to prevent overfitting in neural networks. Overfitting occurs when a model learns not only the useful patterns in the training data but also the noise and irrelevant details, resulting in poor performance on unseen data. Dropout addresses this by randomly setting a fraction of the neurons in the network to zero during each training iteration. This effectively forces the network to learn redundant representations and discourages reliance on any single feature or pathway through the network. The randomness introduced by dropout acts as a form of ensemble learning within a single model. Since different subsets of the network are trained at each iteration, the final model becomes an average of many slightly different models, improving its ability to generalize. The dropout rate, typically set between 0.2 and 0.5, controls how aggressive the regularization is. A higher rate means more neurons are dropped, which can enhance regularization but also hinder learning if too much information is lost.

Batch normalization, in contrast, is not primarily a regularization technique but a method to stabilize and accelerate the training of deep networks. It works by normalizing the inputs of each layer so that they have a mean of zero and a standard deviation of one, calculated across the mini-batch. This normalization helps mitigate the problem of internal covariate shift, where the distribution of layer inputs changes during training as the weights in previous layers are updated. By keeping these distributions stable, batch normalization allows the network to train more efficiently and with less sensitivity to weight initialization and learning rate. It also permits the use of higher learning rates, which can speed up convergence. In addition to normalization, batch normalization includes learnable parameters for scaling and shifting the normalized outputs, preserving the representational power of the network. Interestingly, although it was not designed for regularization, batch normalization often has a regularizing effect and can sometimes reduce or eliminate the need for dropout.

Learning rate schedules provide a dynamic way to control the learning rate during training, adapting it based on progress or performance. The learning rate is one of the most influential hyperparameters in neural network training, dictating how quickly the model updates its weights in response to the gradient of the loss function. A constant learning rate can be suboptimal because what works well in the early stages of training may become too aggressive or too conservative as the model approaches convergence. Learning rate schedules solve this by adjusting the learning rate over time. One common approach is step decay, where the learning rate is reduced by a fixed factor after a predetermined number of epochs. This allows the model to take large steps initially and finer steps later. Another method is exponential decay, where the learning rate is gradually reduced according to an exponential function. More advanced strategies include cosine annealing and cyclical learning rates, which introduce periodic adjustments to the learning rate, helping the model escape local minima and saddle points.

Combining dropout, batch normalization, and learning rate schedules requires careful consideration. While each component improves model performance in different ways, their interactions can affect training dynamics significantly. For instance, dropout introduces noise into the network, which can interfere with the effectiveness of batch normalization, especially if applied directly before or after it. Some practitioners prefer to disable dropout when using batch normalization, relying on the normalization process itself and other regularization methods such as weight decay. Others use both, applying dropout after activation functions and batch normalization in different parts of the architecture to balance their effects. Similarly, learning rate schedules must be chosen with regard to how quickly the model is expected to converge and how sensitive it is to changes in the learning rate. Using an aggressive schedule too early can lead to premature convergence, while a schedule that decays too slowly may result in excessive training time or overfitting.

The effects of these techniques are also influenced by the nature of the dataset and the architecture of the model. In smaller datasets, overfitting is a greater concern, and dropout can be particularly effective. In contrast, for very large datasets, the main challenge is often training efficiency, where batch normalization and appropriate learning rate schedules become more important. Deeper architectures tend to benefit more from batch normalization, as the stabilization of layer inputs reduces the difficulty of training many stacked layers. Recurrent networks and transformers may use variants of these techniques, such as layer normalization instead of batch normalization, and specialized dropout mechanisms that account for the temporal structure of the data.

Implementing these techniques is straightforward in modern deep learning frameworks like TensorFlow and PyTorch, which offer flexible APIs for integrating dropout layers, batch normalization, and learning rate schedulers. However, fine-tuning their parameters and placement within the network architecture requires experimentation and experience. Monitoring training and validation loss curves, inspecting learning rate plots, and using tools such as TensorBoard or Weights and Biases can provide insights into how these components are affecting the training process. For example, sharp spikes in loss after learning rate drops may indicate the need for a smoother schedule, while stagnation in validation accuracy could suggest insufficient regularization or suboptimal batch normalization settings.

Ultimately, dropout, batch normalization, and learning rate schedules are not isolated techniques but part of a cohesive strategy for building effective neural networks. They each address specific challenges in the training process, and when used together, they create a robust environment that encourages efficient learning, prevents overfitting, and enables the model to achieve high levels of generalization. Mastery of these tools requires not just technical understanding but also practical intuition, developed through iterative experimentation and observation of model behavior under different configurations. In the evolving landscape of deep learning, these methods continue to be indispensable components for training stable, accurate, and reliable models across a broad range of applications.

Cross-Validation Strategies for Reliable Tuning

Cross-validation strategies are essential tools for achieving reliable hyperparameter tuning and model evaluation in machine learning. They offer a robust framework for estimating how well a model is likely to perform on unseen data, especially when working with limited datasets or when overfitting is a concern. The core idea behind cross-validation is to partition the available data into subsets that can be used iteratively for training and validation, allowing the model to be evaluated on different segments of the data. This reduces the risk of drawing misleading conclusions based on a single data split and provides a more accurate estimate of a model's generalization ability. Selecting the appropriate cross-validation strategy depends on the nature of the data, the task at hand, and the computational resources available.

The most commonly used method is k-fold cross-validation. In this approach, the dataset is divided into k equally sized folds or subsets. The model is trained on k minus one of these folds and validated on the remaining fold. This process is repeated k times, with each fold serving as the validation set once. The performance metrics from each iteration are then averaged to produce a final estimate. K-fold cross-validation offers a balance between computational efficiency and statistical reliability, especially when k is set to values like five or ten. It ensures that each data point is used both for training and validation, making the evaluation less dependent on any particular partitioning of the data. However, it assumes that the data is independently and identically distributed, which may not be valid for all types of data.

When working with time series or data with temporal dependencies, standard k-fold cross-validation is not appropriate because it allows information from the future to influence the model's training, violating the chronological order of events. In such cases, time series cross-validation, also known as forward chaining or rolling-origin validation, is used. This method maintains the temporal structure by training on a growing window of past observations and validating on a future segment. For example, the model is first trained on the first portion of the data and tested on the next chunk. In subsequent iterations, more past data is included in training, while the validation window moves forward. This simulates the real-world scenario where predictions are made on future data using historical information and ensures that no leakage occurs across the training-validation boundary.

Another variation, stratified k-fold cross-validation, is particularly useful for classification tasks with imbalanced class distributions. In stratified k-fold, the splitting process ensures that each fold maintains the original class proportions, providing a more representative sample in each fold. This is especially important when the target class of interest appears infrequently in the dataset. Without stratification, some folds might contain very few or even none of the minority class instances, leading to skewed and unreliable performance estimates. By preserving class ratios, stratified k-fold helps produce consistent and fair evaluations that reflect the model's ability to detect all classes adequately.

For very small datasets, leave-one-out cross-validation offers an alternative that maximizes data usage. In this method, the model is trained on all data points except one and validated on the excluded point. This process is repeated for each data point in the dataset. While this method provides nearly unbiased estimates, it is computationally expensive and can suffer from high variance, particularly if the data is noisy. Each model is trained on nearly identical data, which can lead to overfitting to slight differences in individual observations. Despite these limitations, leave-one-out remains a valuable strategy in cases where the number of available samples is extremely limited, and using as much data as possible for training is a priority.

Nested cross-validation is an advanced strategy used when both model evaluation and hyperparameter tuning must be performed reliably. It involves two layers of cross-validation: an outer loop for assessing model performance and an inner loop for tuning hyperparameters. This approach prevents data leakage between the tuning process and the final performance evaluation. In the inner loop, the best hyperparameters are selected based on validation folds, and in the outer loop, the model with those hyperparameters is evaluated on previously unseen data. This layered structure provides an unbiased estimate of how well the tuned model is likely to perform in real-world scenarios. Although nested cross-validation is computationally intensive, it is indispensable for rigorous model selection, especially in academic and high-stakes applications where robust evaluation is critical.

Repeated cross-validation further enhances reliability by repeating the k-fold process multiple times with different random splits of the data. Each repetition introduces a new division of the data into folds, reducing the sensitivity of the evaluation to a particular data split. The final performance metrics are averaged across all repetitions, producing a more stable estimate. Repeated cross-validation is especially useful in situations where the dataset is not large enough to ensure that a single split is representative or where the model performance varies significantly depending on the training data. Although more expensive computationally, it offers increased confidence in the evaluation and tuning process.

Cross-validation can also be adapted to specific use cases, such as group k-fold for data with clustered or grouped observations. In this method, entire groups are held out for validation, ensuring that the model is tested on truly independent samples. This is common in medical data, where patients may contribute multiple records, or in recommendation systems, where interactions from the same user or item should not be split between training and validation. By respecting these group boundaries, group k-fold prevents leakage of information and produces more realistic estimates of model performance in production settings.

One must also consider the impact of cross-validation on computational cost. Since cross-validation involves training and validating the model multiple times, it can be time-consuming, especially for complex models or large datasets. Efficient implementations and parallel processing can mitigate some of these costs, but it remains important to balance thoroughness with practical constraints. In some cases, a simple train-test split may suffice for preliminary experiments, with more robust cross-validation reserved for final model selection and evaluation.

Cross-validation strategies are deeply intertwined with hyperparameter tuning, as they provide the framework for assessing the performance of different configurations. Whether using grid search, random search, or more advanced optimization techniques like Bayesian optimization, cross-validation ensures that the selected parameters are not just optimal for a specific data split but generalize well across different subsets. Without a sound cross-validation strategy, tuning efforts can result in models that perform well during development but fail in deployment. Therefore, selecting and implementing the right cross-validation approach is not a secondary consideration but a foundational element of reliable model development and evaluation.

Early Stopping and Model Convergence

Early stopping and model convergence are two intertwined concepts that play a crucial role in ensuring that machine learning models, particularly deep learning models, achieve high performance without overfitting. Training a model is essentially an optimization problem where the objective is to minimize a loss function, guiding the model parameters towards values that best explain the training data. As the optimization algorithm proceeds, the loss typically decreases, and model performance on the training set improves. However, continual improvement on the training set does not necessarily translate into better performance on unseen data. This is where early stopping becomes essential, serving as a practical and effective form of regularization that halts training at the point where the model begins to overfit the training data.

Model convergence refers to the point in training where further iterations yield minimal or no improvements in the loss function. Ideally, a model converges when it has found a set of parameters that minimize the loss not just on the training data but also on validation data. However, the path to convergence is not always smooth. Depending on the learning rate, initialization, and the complexity of the model, training can stall in local minima, oscillate due to high gradients, or continue to reduce training loss while degrading generalization. Early stopping leverages a validation set to monitor the model's generalization error, allowing training to terminate once performance on this held-out data ceases to improve, even if the training loss continues to decrease.

The typical implementation of early stopping involves tracking a specific metric on the validation set—commonly loss, accuracy, or some task-specific performance measure—at the end of each epoch. If the validation metric does not improve for a specified number of consecutive epochs, known as the patience parameter, training is halted. The model parameters corresponding to the best observed validation performance are then restored. This approach prevents the model from wasting computational resources on training epochs that offer no benefit and shields it from learning patterns that are specific to the noise or peculiarities of the training set.

Choosing the patience parameter is critical. If patience is too short, the training may stop prematurely before the model has had a chance to fully learn the underlying structure of the data. If it is too long, the model might overfit despite the mechanism in place. The right setting depends on factors such as the size of the dataset, the complexity of the model, the volatility of the validation metric, and the learning rate. In practice, it is often determined empirically, sometimes through a few trial runs or combined with visualization of learning curves to observe when validation performance plateaus.

Early stopping is closely tied to learning rate selection. A higher learning rate can speed up convergence but may also cause fluctuations in the validation metric, making it difficult to detect genuine improvement. A lower learning rate results in smoother training but might delay the point at which performance starts to degrade. Because early stopping depends on recognizing a plateau or degradation in validation performance, setting an appropriate learning rate helps ensure that these patterns are clear and distinguishable. This interaction underscores the importance of considering early stopping not in isolation but as part of a broader training strategy involving learning rate schedules and optimizer settings.

Another aspect of early stopping is its role in model selection and hyperparameter tuning. When combined with cross-validation or nested cross-validation, early stopping allows models to be evaluated under realistic conditions that reflect the performance they are likely to achieve in production. It ensures that comparisons among models or hyperparameter settings are not biased by overfitting, as each model is evaluated at its own optimal stopping point rather than after a fixed number of epochs. This dynamic evaluation capability enhances the reliability and reproducibility of machine learning experiments.

In neural networks, especially deep ones, the risk of overfitting increases with model capacity. The more parameters a model has, the more prone it is to memorize training data instead of generalizing patterns. While dropout, batch normalization, and weight decay are common regularization techniques used to mitigate this issue, early stopping adds an additional layer of protection. It effectively sets a cap on the model's learning capacity, adapting to the specific dataset and task. This adaptability makes it especially useful in cases where the data is noisy, the labels are uncertain, or the amount of data is limited.

Early stopping also improves training efficiency by reducing unnecessary computation. Instead of completing a predefined number of epochs, which might be arbitrary or overly conservative, the training process ends as soon as it becomes unproductive. This reduction in computation is particularly valuable when training on large datasets or using complex architectures that require significant resources. It also shortens the iteration cycle for experimentation, allowing data scientists and researchers to test more configurations in less time and focus their efforts on promising models.

One of the subtleties of early stopping is its dependence on a reliable validation set. If the validation set is not representative of the data distribution, the stopping decision may be misleading. The validation set must be drawn independently of the training data and should reflect the same statistical properties as the eventual test or deployment environment. Any contamination between the training and validation sets can compromise the effectiveness of early stopping and result in overly optimistic performance estimates. It is also important to ensure that the validation metric is meaningful for the specific problem, as poor metric choice can lead to suboptimal stopping points and underperforming models.

In some implementations, early stopping is extended with checkpointing, where model weights are periodically saved and the best version according to the validation metric is preserved. This safeguard ensures that even if the training is interrupted or if subsequent epochs degrade performance, the optimal model is not lost. Checkpointing is especially useful when training models over extended periods or across distributed systems where stability and fault tolerance are essential.

The concept of model convergence continues to evolve with advances in optimization algorithms and training techniques. For example, newer methods like one-cycle learning rate policies or adaptive gradient clipping influence how quickly and stably a model converges. These methods, when combined with early stopping, offer more controlled and efficient pathways to optimal models. Convergence is no longer viewed solely as minimizing a static loss function but as achieving a balance between learning sufficient complexity and maintaining generalization, all within the practical limits of computational resources and data availability.

Ultimately, early stopping and model convergence are about making intelligent decisions during training. They allow models to reach their best possible performance while avoiding the pitfalls of overfitting and excessive computation. They introduce a dynamic, data-driven mechanism for deciding when learning has achieved its goal and provide a framework for controlling model complexity in a principled and adaptive way. For practitioners aiming to develop models that are not only accurate but also efficient and robust, mastering these concepts is a vital step toward building high-quality machine learning systems.

Automated Machine Learning and Feature Engineering

Automated Machine Learning, commonly known as AutoML, represents a significant evolution in the practice of building machine learning models. It aims to reduce the manual labor, technical expertise, and time typically required for designing and deploying effective models. One of the most complex and impactful components of the machine learning workflow is feature engineering, the process of transforming raw data into inputs that enable models to perform well. Traditionally, feature engineering has been a labor-intensive task requiring domain expertise, creativity, and iterative experimentation. AutoML platforms have introduced ways to automate parts or even the entirety of this process, enabling faster development cycles and expanding access to machine learning to non-experts. The integration of automated feature engineering into AutoML systems has become one of its most transformative contributions.

Feature engineering is at the heart of any predictive modeling task. Raw data, in its original form, is often noisy, unstructured, and unsuitable for immediate consumption by algorithms. This data must be cleaned, structured, and encoded in a way that reveals relevant patterns while suppressing noise and redundancy. Features might include simple statistical summaries, such as averages and counts, or more complex transformations like time lags, polynomial interactions, or textual embeddings. A well-engineered feature set can drastically improve model accuracy, robustness, and interpretability. In traditional workflows, data scientists manually select which features to create based on experience and iterative feedback from model performance metrics. This manual loop is slow, subjective, and hard to scale.

AutoML platforms attempt to standardize and automate this loop by employing algorithmic approaches that search for optimal feature transformations, combinations, and selections. At its core, automated feature engineering seeks to identify the representations of input data that maximize a model's predictive performance with minimal human intervention. This is achieved through the use of heuristic methods, meta-learning, statistical testing, and model-based evaluation. Systems like FeatureTools, TransmogrifAI, and built-in tools within platforms such as Google AutoML or H2O.ai are capable of generating new features by automatically analyzing the structure of the data, identifying relationships between columns, and applying a library of transformations.

One common technique in automated feature engineering is deep feature synthesis. This approach constructs new features by stacking multiple operations over primitive input variables. For example, in a retail dataset, it might combine a customer ID with purchase timestamps to create a new feature such as average purchase frequency or time since last transaction. These synthesized features can capture complex relationships that would be difficult to identify manually. Deep feature synthesis operates by iteratively applying aggregation and transformation functions across related entities in relational data. This allows AutoML tools to handle multi-table datasets effectively, something that has traditionally required significant domain-specific SQL coding and data manipulation skills.

Another critical aspect of automated feature engineering is handling categorical variables, missing data, and variable scaling. AutoML systems automate encoding techniques such as one-hot encoding, label encoding, or target encoding, depending on the modeling algorithm and the statistical characteristics of the feature. For missing values, strategies such as imputation using mean, median, or more advanced model-based imputation are selected automatically based on what improves downstream performance. Numerical features are often scaled using standardization or normalization, and AutoML tools test multiple scaling methods to find the one most suited to the specific algorithm in use, whether it be logistic regression, random forests, or neural networks.

Beyond transformation and imputation, feature selection is another area where automation significantly enhances the modeling process. Not all features contribute positively to model performance, and some may introduce noise or multicollinearity. AutoML pipelines incorporate feature selection techniques to identify and retain only the most informative features. These methods range from univariate statistical tests to recursive feature elimination and embedded methods based on feature importance metrics from models like XGBoost or LightGBM. By continuously evaluating model performance as features are added or removed, AutoML systems can converge on a feature set that balances accuracy, simplicity, and generalization.

Automated feature engineering does not exist in isolation but is often integrated into broader AutoML pipelines that also include model selection, hyperparameter tuning, and evaluation. These pipelines operate as nested loops where different feature sets are tested against a variety of models, with feedback used to refine both feature and model configurations. The interaction between feature engineering and model choice is complex. Some models, like decision trees, are robust to unscaled and non-linear features, while others, like linear models or neural networks, require specific types of preprocessing. AutoML systems learn these interactions through internal performance tracking, often guided by meta-learning strategies that leverage knowledge from previous tasks to make better decisions on new ones.

Interpretability is an important consideration in automated feature engineering. Although automation can uncover complex patterns and interactions, the resulting models may be harder to explain to stakeholders if the features are abstract or highly transformed. Advanced AutoML tools provide insights into which features contributed most to the predictions, often using SHAP values, permutation importance, or partial dependence plots. These interpretability modules help bridge the gap between automation and transparency, ensuring that automated decisions can be scrutinized and trusted. This is especially critical in regulated industries like healthcare or finance, where explainability is not optional but a legal and ethical necessity.

Automated feature engineering is particularly valuable in scenarios involving large-scale data or when rapid prototyping is required. In hackathons, early-stage projects, or business environments where decisions need to be made quickly, AutoML allows teams to deliver functioning models in hours rather than weeks. It democratizes machine learning by enabling domain experts without deep technical backgrounds to develop predictive systems using their knowledge of the problem, while the system handles the complexity of feature generation and selection. This efficiency also supports experimentation at scale, allowing multiple modeling approaches to be tested in parallel without manual overhead.

Despite its power, automated feature engineering is not without challenges. There is always a risk that important domain knowledge may be lost if human oversight is completely removed. AutoML systems are only as good as the assumptions and libraries they are built on. In some cases, critical context-dependent features cannot be synthesized from data alone and require human insight. Moreover, the computational cost of generating and testing hundreds or thousands of feature combinations can be significant, necessitating high-performance infrastructure or cloud-based solutions.

Nevertheless, the growing sophistication of AutoML and automated feature engineering tools continues to push the boundaries of what is possible in applied machine learning. They are reshaping the way models are developed, shifting focus from manual, trial-and-error processes to streamlined, data-driven pipelines. As these systems evolve, they promise to further reduce the gap between data and decisions, allowing machine learning to be applied more widely, rapidly, and responsibly across industries.

Feature Importance Metrics in Tree Models

Feature importance metrics in tree models are powerful tools that provide insights into how machine learning algorithms make predictions based on input variables. Decision trees and their ensemble variants, such as random forests and gradient boosted trees, have the unique advantage of being inherently interpretable due to their structure. These models split data based on feature values, making them well-suited for identifying which variables contribute most significantly to predictions. Understanding feature importance is not just a matter of curiosity; it is fundamental to improving model performance, debugging errors, reducing dimensionality, and gaining domain-specific insights from data. These metrics help quantify the relative contribution of each feature and play a crucial role in both model diagnostics and trustworthiness.

In tree-based models, one of the most common methods for measuring feature importance is based on the reduction in impurity that results from a split. Impurity can be measured using different criteria depending on the task—Gini impurity and entropy are typical in classification problems, while mean squared error is used in regression tasks. Each time a node in a tree splits on a feature, it reduces the impurity of the resulting child nodes compared to the parent node. This reduction is attributed to the feature used for the split. By summing the impurity reductions across all nodes where a feature is used and averaging it over all trees in an ensemble, a global measure of feature importance can be derived. This approach, known as mean decrease in impurity, is simple to implement and computationally efficient, which makes it widely used in libraries like scikit-learn.

However, impurity-based feature importance has limitations. It tends to favor features with many unique values or high cardinality, such as continuous variables or categorical variables with many levels. These features offer more potential split points, increasing the likelihood that they will appear in the tree, even if they are not truly informative. As a result, models may overemphasize these features, misleading users about their true predictive power. Furthermore, when two features are correlated, the model may use only one of them repeatedly while assigning little or no importance to the other, even if both are equally relevant. This can obscure relationships in the data and reduce transparency.

To address the limitations of impurity-based metrics, permutation importance offers a more robust alternative. This method evaluates the importance of a feature by measuring how much the model's performance deteriorates when the feature's values are randomly shuffled. The idea is that if a feature is truly important, disrupting its relationship with the target variable should significantly degrade the model's accuracy or other performance metric. Permutation importance is model-agnostic and can be applied to any predictive model, not just tree-based ones. In the context of tree models, it often yields more reliable results because it considers the actual influence of a feature on predictions, rather than relying solely on structural statistics.

Despite its advantages, permutation importance also has challenges. It is computationally expensive, especially for large datasets or complex models, because it requires retraining or re-evaluating the model multiple times. It is also sensitive to feature correlations. When features are correlated, shuffling one may not lead to a substantial drop in performance because the model can rely on the correlated feature as a proxy. This can result in underestimating the importance of both features, again obscuring their true role in the prediction process. To mitigate this, conditional permutation importance methods have been proposed, which attempt to shuffle feature values while preserving their relationships with other variables. This approach provides a more accurate measure of feature relevance in the presence of multicollinearity.

Another increasingly popular metric is SHAP, or SHapley Additive exPlanations. SHAP values are grounded in cooperative game theory and aim to fairly distribute the contribution of each feature to a given prediction. Unlike global importance measures, SHAP provides both global and local interpretability, showing not only which features are important on average but also how each feature influenced the prediction for a specific instance. In tree-based models, TreeSHAP is an optimized algorithm that computes exact SHAP values efficiently by leveraging the structure of decision trees. This has made SHAP a widely accepted tool for interpreting models built with frameworks like XGBoost, LightGBM, and CatBoost.

The advantage of SHAP is its consistency and theoretical foundation. If a model changes in a way that increases the contribution of a feature, the SHAP value for that feature also increases, maintaining logical consistency. SHAP also captures interaction effects between features, which traditional importance metrics may miss. For example, two features may individually have little impact but jointly explain a significant part of the variance. SHAP can reveal these relationships by attributing shared contributions appropriately. However, the complexity of SHAP and the need for significant computational resources in very large datasets remain practical concerns, especially when models are retrained frequently or deployed in real-time systems.

In addition to SHAP, other methods such as partial dependence plots and accumulated local effects provide visual insights into how features influence model predictions. While not strictly importance metrics, these tools complement importance scores by showing whether a feature has a linear, monotonic, or more complex relationship with the target. In tree models, where non-linearity and interactions are common, these plots help contextualize importance rankings by offering intuitive explanations of feature behavior. They also assist in validating whether the model has learned sensible patterns or has picked up on spurious correlations that could lead to unexpected predictions.

Evaluating feature importance is not only about ranking variables but also about supporting better decision-making in downstream tasks. In high-dimensional datasets, for instance, removing features with low importance scores can simplify models, reduce overfitting, and improve computational efficiency. In applications such as finance, healthcare, or policy-making, understanding which variables drive decisions is critical for transparency, fairness, and accountability. Feature importance metrics help detect potential biases, ensure compliance with ethical guidelines, and build trust with users and stakeholders.

It is important to remember that feature importance reflects the data used to train the model. If the training data is biased, incomplete, or unrepresentative, the importance scores may reflect these issues rather than true causal relationships. Continuous monitoring, validation with domain experts, and incorporation of causal inference methods are necessary to move from importance to insight. Feature importance metrics in tree models provide a valuable starting point for this journey, combining interpretability with performance in a way that bridges the gap between data science and real-world impact. As models become more complex and data more abundant, the role of these metrics will only grow in importance, guiding the development of machine learning systems that are not only powerful but also understandable and responsible.

SHAP and LIME for Model Interpretability

SHAP and LIME are two of the most widely used techniques in the domain of model interpretability, especially for complex machine learning models that function as black boxes. As machine learning models become more sophisticated and are deployed in high-stakes environments such as healthcare, finance, and criminal justice, the need to explain their predictions becomes increasingly important. Stakeholders must understand why a model made a certain prediction, whether that decision is fair, and how to trust the model's output. SHAP, short for SHapley Additive exPlanations, and LIME, which stands for Local Interpretable Model-agnostic Explanations, provide powerful tools to make opaque models transparent, helping users gain insights into individual predictions and global model behavior.

LIME operates by approximating the local decision boundary of a complex model with a simpler, interpretable model such as a linear regression or decision tree. To do this, LIME perturbs the input data around a specific instance and observes how the model's predictions change in response. By generating many such perturbations and recording their corresponding outputs, LIME fits a surrogate model that captures the local behavior of the original model in the vicinity of the instance. The coefficients of this local surrogate model then act as explanations, showing which features were most influential in determining the prediction. This approach provides human-readable insights that are easy to understand, making it popular among practitioners seeking a quick and intuitive method to explain model outputs.

However, LIME comes with limitations. Since the explanations are based on a local approximation, the fidelity of the explanation depends on how accurately the surrogate model mimics the complex model in the perturbed space. If the complex model has highly non-linear or irregular behavior, the local surrogate may fail to capture its nuances, leading to misleading explanations. Additionally, LIME's reliance on randomly generated perturbations can result in variability between runs, making the explanations less stable. The choice of kernel, neighborhood size, and number of samples all affect the outcome, and selecting these hyperparameters requires careful consideration to ensure consistent and meaningful explanations.

SHAP addresses some of these challenges by offering a theoretically grounded approach to attribution based on cooperative game theory. At the heart of SHAP lies the concept of Shapley values, a solution from game theory that fairly distributes the payout among players depending on their individual contributions to the total outcome. In the context of machine learning, features are treated as players in a coalition, and the goal is to assign each feature a value that represents its contribution to the prediction. SHAP calculates these contributions by considering all possible combinations of feature subsets and measuring how the inclusion or exclusion of a feature changes the model output. The resulting SHAP values provide a comprehensive view of how each feature impacts a specific prediction.

One of the most appealing properties of SHAP is its consistency. If a model changes in such a way that a feature contributes more to the prediction, the SHAP value for that feature also increases. This ensures logical coherence in the attribution process, something not guaranteed by all interpretability methods. SHAP values are also additive, meaning that the sum of the feature attributions equals the model's prediction minus the expected value of the prediction across the entire dataset. This additivity enables clear and complete decomposition of individual predictions, which is critical in high-stakes settings where every detail must be accounted for and justified.

There are different variants of SHAP tailored to specific model types. TreeSHAP is optimized for decision tree-based models like random forests, XGBoost, and LightGBM, allowing for exact SHAP value computation with high efficiency. DeepSHAP extends the concept to deep learning models by leveraging connections with DeepLIFT, a method for propagating contribution scores through neural networks. KernelSHAP is the model-agnostic variant that can be applied to any predictive model, though it is computationally intensive because it relies on sampling and approximations to estimate Shapley values. Regardless of the variant, SHAP offers detailed explanations at both the local level, for individual predictions, and the global level, by aggregating SHAP values across many instances to reveal feature importance and interactions.

In practice, SHAP explanations are often visualized through force plots, summary plots, dependence plots, and decision plots. These visualizations help users not only see which features are important but also understand the direction and magnitude of their influence. A force plot, for instance, shows how individual features push a prediction higher or lower relative to the baseline. A summary plot aggregates this information across multiple instances to display the global influence of features. Dependence plots go further by illustrating how a feature's value relates to its SHAP value, highlighting non-linear patterns and interactions. These tools transform raw SHAP values into interpretable insights that are actionable and intuitive.

While SHAP offers many advantages, it is not without trade-offs. Computing SHAP values, especially with KernelSHAP, can be computationally expensive, particularly on large datasets with many features. The requirement to evaluate the model on numerous perturbed feature sets can lead to long runtimes, making it challenging for real-time applications. Moreover, while SHAP provides faithful representations of feature contributions, its interpretability can diminish when dealing with hundreds or thousands of features, as users may struggle to extract actionable insights from such high-dimensional explanations. In these scenarios, combining SHAP with feature selection or dimensionality reduction techniques can help focus attention on the most relevant aspects of the model.

Both SHAP and LIME play complementary roles in the model interpretability ecosystem. LIME is lightweight, fast, and easy to implement, making it ideal for prototyping and gaining initial insights. It is especially useful when rapid explanations are needed or when the model is too complex to allow SHAP to run efficiently. SHAP, on the other hand, offers deeper theoretical guarantees, consistent attributions, and richer explanations, which are valuable in production environments and regulatory contexts. Choosing between SHAP and LIME depends on the specific requirements of the task, the nature of the model, and the computational constraints.

Model interpretability is no longer optional in machine learning practice. As algorithms take on roles that impact human lives, it is essential to ensure that their decisions are transparent, explainable, and aligned with ethical standards. SHAP and LIME have emerged as leading solutions to this need, enabling practitioners to open the black box of machine learning and reveal the logic behind the predictions. They empower users to question, verify, and improve models, ultimately fostering trust and accountability in automated decision-making systems. As machine learning continues to evolve, these interpretability tools will remain essential, not only for understanding models but also for guiding their responsible and effective deployment in the real world.

Feature Drift Detection and Updating

Feature drift detection and updating are critical processes in maintaining the performance and reliability of machine learning models deployed in real-world environments. While models are typically trained on historical data, the real world is dynamic. Over time, the distributions of input features can shift, sometimes subtly and sometimes dramatically. This phenomenon is known as feature drift or covariate shift, and if it goes undetected, it can cause models to degrade, leading to poor predictions and potentially harmful decisions. Feature drift does not necessarily imply that the relationship between inputs and outputs has changed, but it does indicate that the assumptions made during training no longer fully hold. Continuous monitoring, detection, and adaptive updates are essential to ensure that models remain accurate, trustworthy, and aligned with the current state of data.

Feature drift can arise from numerous sources. In business contexts, user behavior might evolve due to changing market trends, seasonal patterns, or the introduction of new products. In sensor-based systems, hardware upgrades, environmental changes, or calibration issues can affect the input signals. In healthcare, shifts in patient demographics or medical practices can alter the statistical properties of input features. Regardless of the source, any change in the feature distribution that differs from what the model was trained on can compromise its predictions. Feature drift differs from concept drift, where the relationship between inputs and outputs changes. However, both often co-occur and require robust monitoring strategies to handle effectively.

Detecting feature drift involves statistical comparisons between distributions over time. A common approach is to compare the distribution of a feature in the training dataset with its distribution in recent production data. Several statistical tests are available for this purpose. The Kolmogorov-Smirnov test, for example, is a nonparametric test that compares the empirical distribution functions of two samples and quantifies the maximum distance between them. It is suitable for continuous variables and helps determine whether a feature has changed significantly. For categorical variables, the chi-squared test is often used to assess whether observed frequencies deviate from expected frequencies. More advanced methods include the Population Stability Index, Kullback-Leibler divergence, and Wasserstein distance, each with its own strengths and limitations depending on the data type and context.

Machine learning systems can incorporate automated monitoring pipelines that regularly evaluate these statistical metrics and trigger alerts when drift is detected. These pipelines often involve time-windowed monitoring, where feature distributions are compared over rolling intervals to capture both sudden and gradual shifts. It is essential to define thresholds that distinguish between normal variability and meaningful drift. This involves balancing sensitivity and specificity to avoid false positives that lead to unnecessary interventions or false negatives that allow drift to go undetected. Visualization tools such as histograms, density plots, and cumulative distribution functions are often used in conjunction with statistical tests to support human-in-the-loop interpretation and decision-making.

Once feature drift has been detected, the next step is updating the model or its components to address the changes. The most straightforward strategy is to retrain the model using recent data that reflects the current distribution. This can be done periodically or triggered by drift detection events. Retraining may involve replacing the entire training dataset with fresh data or appending recent data to the existing dataset, followed by re-optimization of the model parameters. The frequency and scope of retraining depend on factors such as data volatility, model complexity, and operational constraints. While retraining is effective, it is also resource-intensive and may not be feasible in all situations.

An alternative to full retraining is incremental learning, where models are updated continuously or in small batches as new data becomes available. Online learning algorithms such as stochastic gradient descent can adjust model weights in real-time, making them well-suited for streaming data and environments with frequent drift. Ensemble methods, too, offer flexibility in handling drift. Models can be trained on different time slices of the data, and the ensemble can be dynamically re-weighted or refreshed to emphasize more recent models. These techniques allow systems to adapt gradually without requiring full retraining from scratch.

In some cases, the features themselves need to be updated or engineered differently to maintain model performance. For example, if a feature becomes less informative or begins to correlate differently with the target, it may be necessary to create new derived features, normalize differently, or replace the affected variable entirely. This process may also include re-evaluating the importance of features through permutation importance, SHAP values, or other explainability tools. Feature selection mechanisms can then identify which variables remain relevant under the new data distribution. This continuous re-engineering of features ensures that the model adapts not only in parameters but also in how it interprets the incoming data.

Feature drift detection and updating also raise broader concerns about system governance, accountability, and fairness. When features change, the implications may go beyond technical performance. For instance, if a model used in credit scoring begins to rely more heavily on features that correlate with sensitive attributes like race or gender due to drift, it could unintentionally introduce bias or discrimination. Therefore, drift detection should be integrated with fairness and compliance monitoring frameworks. It is also important to document drift-related updates and communicate changes to stakeholders, especially in regulated industries where transparency is required.

Model validation in the presence of drift must also be adapted. Traditional validation methods, which assume that training and validation data come from the same distribution, may no longer be valid if drift is present. Time-based cross-validation or forward chaining methods can provide more realistic estimates of future performance under evolving data conditions. Moreover, validation strategies should be recalibrated each time the model or its feature set is updated. Continuous evaluation on live data, along with shadow models that run in parallel to production systems without influencing outcomes, can provide ongoing performance assessments and support safe deployment of updates.

Drift-aware systems are becoming an essential component of machine learning operations. As models are deployed into dynamic environments, the ability to detect, interpret, and respond to feature drift determines their long-term viability. Rather than treating models as static artifacts, practitioners must embrace a lifecycle approach in which models are monitored, maintained, and evolved in response to changing data. Automated pipelines that integrate drift detection with retraining, validation, and deployment create resilient systems capable of sustaining high performance. Feature drift, when managed effectively, does not have to be a threat. It becomes a signal—an indication that the world has changed and that the model must grow alongside it.

Feature Engineering in Production Pipelines

Feature engineering in production pipelines is one of the most critical components of building robust, scalable, and maintainable machine learning systems. While many view feature engineering as a purely exploratory task confined to the early stages of model development, its role in production environments is far more complex and consequential. Moving a machine learning model from a research setting to production requires that every transformation applied to the raw data during training be precisely replicated in real-time, often under strict latency, reliability, and consistency constraints. Any deviation between the training and inference environments, even in a single feature, can lead to catastrophic drops in model performance and reliability, undermining the credibility of the entire system. For this reason, feature engineering must be treated as a first-class citizen within the architecture of a production machine learning pipeline.

In a production context, feature engineering must be automated, reproducible, and versioned. Unlike in development, where analysts and data scientists might experiment with ad hoc transformations in notebooks, production systems require formalized pipelines that are deployed as code. These pipelines must read incoming data, perform all necessary cleaning, normalization, encoding, and aggregation steps, and deliver the resulting features to the model in a format that matches the expectations established during training. This consistency is crucial because any mismatch can lead to silent failures that are hard to detect. For example, if a categorical variable is one-hot encoded during training with a certain set of categories, and a new unseen category appears in production, the feature vector's shape or semantics can change unexpectedly. Handling such edge cases is a key responsibility of production-grade feature engineering pipelines.

Scalability is another major consideration. In production environments, machine learning systems often operate at scale, serving predictions for thousands or even millions of users in real-time. This requires that feature transformations be not only correct but also computationally efficient. Operations that are acceptable in batch training environments, such as sorting, joins, or large-scale aggregations, may be too slow or memory-intensive to perform in real-time. As a result, production pipelines must often be re-engineered to use approximate or precomputed features, caching strategies, or streaming architectures that can handle data incrementally. This introduces a significant engineering challenge: maintaining the logical equivalence of features between training and serving while optimizing for performance.

One common solution to this problem is the use of feature stores. A feature store is a centralized system for managing feature definitions, computation, storage, and retrieval. It enables teams to define features once and use them consistently across both training and serving environments. Feature stores support batch and real-time feature generation and provide tooling for version control, lineage tracking, and monitoring. This ensures that models receive the same features during inference as they did during training, eliminating one of the most common sources of production bugs in machine learning systems. Feature stores also promote reusability and collaboration across teams, as well-engineered features can be shared and reused across multiple models and applications.

Latency is a critical metric in production systems, especially in applications such as recommendation engines, fraud detection, and personalized search, where predictions must be delivered in milliseconds. Feature engineering pipelines must be optimized to meet these latency requirements. This often involves precomputing expensive features offline and storing them for fast retrieval, or engineering real-time features using efficient algorithms that operate on streams of incoming events. Time-based features, such as recency scores or rolling averages, are particularly challenging because they depend on up-to-date information. Maintaining these features in real-time requires stream processing frameworks and careful management of stateful computations, windowing strategies, and out-of-order data handling.

Robustness and fault tolerance are equally important. In production, data pipelines can break for a variety of reasons: schema changes, missing data, upstream service failures, or corrupted inputs. Feature engineering pipelines must be resilient to these issues. This involves implementing safeguards such as schema validation, null handling, imputation strategies, and fallbacks for missing features. Monitoring and alerting are essential components of this system. It is critical to track not only model performance but also the quality and distribution of input features over time. Sudden shifts in feature distributions, known as feature drift, can be early indicators of data quality issues or underlying changes in user behavior that require retraining or feature adjustments.

Security and privacy concerns also shape how feature engineering is conducted in production. Features that involve sensitive user data must comply with privacy regulations such as GDPR or HIPAA. This means enforcing data minimization, encryption, and access control policies throughout the pipeline. In some cases, differential privacy techniques may be applied to prevent the leakage of individual-level information. Feature engineering must respect these constraints, ensuring that no personally identifiable information is exposed or misused during training or inference. This adds an additional layer of complexity to the pipeline but is essential for building trustworthy and compliant machine learning systems.

Deployment and testing of feature engineering logic must follow software engineering best practices. This includes writing unit tests for transformation functions, integration tests for pipeline components, and end-to-end tests that validate the entire flow from raw input to final prediction. Continuous integration and deployment pipelines should automatically run these tests to catch regressions or compatibility issues before changes reach production. Code for feature engineering should be modular, documented, and version-controlled, enabling reproducibility and collaborative development. As models are retrained or updated, changes to feature definitions must be tracked, and old versions must be preserved to support model rollback or forensic analysis.

Lastly, observability is crucial for maintaining feature engineering pipelines in production. It is not enough to monitor model outputs;

engineers must also track feature availability, freshness, and distribution over time. This includes logging feature values, monitoring update frequencies, and generating alerts for anomalies. Dashboards and automated reports help teams visualize the health of their pipelines and make informed decisions about maintenance and retraining. When models behave unexpectedly, these observability tools provide the data necessary to diagnose whether the root cause lies in the features, the model, or the input data itself.

Feature engineering in production is where the theoretical meets the practical. It is not only about creating features that improve accuracy but also about designing systems that are stable, performant, and maintainable under real-world conditions. The best features are not just informative—they are reliable, efficient, and deliverable at scale. Building these systems requires close collaboration between data scientists, data engineers, and software developers, and a deep understanding of both the data and the operational constraints of the production environment. In the end, it is this fusion of statistical insight and engineering discipline that enables machine learning models to make a lasting impact beyond the lab and into the hands of users.

Scalable Feature Engineering with Big Data Tools

Scalable feature engineering with big data tools is a fundamental necessity in modern data science workflows, especially when dealing with datasets that exceed the capacity of single machines. As organizations collect vast amounts of data from logs, sensors, transactions, and user interactions, the challenge shifts from simply developing features to doing so efficiently and reliably at scale. Traditional tools such as pandas or Excel, while effective for small to medium datasets, quickly become inadequate when data reaches terabytes or petabytes. At this scale, distributed computing frameworks and big data processing platforms are essential to extract meaningful features without compromising on performance or reliability.

Apache Spark is one of the most widely used big data tools for scalable feature engineering. Its distributed architecture allows data processing tasks to be spread across multiple nodes, enabling parallel computation over massive datasets. Spark's DataFrame API and SQL-like syntax provide an accessible interface for manipulating structured data, while its underlying execution engine optimizes operations through lazy evaluation and query planning. Feature transformations such as joins, aggregations, groupings, and window functions can all be expressed declaratively in Spark and executed efficiently across a cluster. This makes it possible to perform complex feature engineering tasks, such as calculating rolling averages, extracting time-based features, or encoding categorical variables, on billions of rows with relatively minimal infrastructure overhead.

One of the most powerful aspects of Spark is its integration with machine learning pipelines through MLlib. Spark ML pipelines allow data scientists to define feature engineering steps as a sequence of transformations that can be applied consistently during both training and inference. These pipelines support operations like tokenization, hashing, normalization, standardization, and one-hot encoding, and they can be composed modularly to form end-to-end workflows. When these workflows are persisted and versioned, they offer a reliable mechanism for reproducing feature generation across different environments, ensuring that features used during training are identical to those used in production inference systems.

Apache Beam is another versatile tool that supports unified batch and stream processing, making it ideal for scenarios where features must be computed in real time or near real time. Beam's portability across runners such as Apache Flink, Google Cloud Dataflow, and Spark gives teams the flexibility to choose the right execution environment based on scale, latency, and cost considerations. With Beam, feature engineering logic can be defined once and executed in different modes depending on the business need. For example, aggregating user click behavior over a thirty-minute window can be computed in streaming mode for real-time recommendation systems or in batch mode for periodic model retraining. This unification reduces code duplication and helps ensure consistency between offline and online features.

Hadoop and its ecosystem, including Hive and Pig, played a foundational role in making big data processing accessible, and while some newer technologies have surpassed it in performance and flexibility, they still serve a purpose in many legacy systems. Hive, for instance, allows SQL-like queries to be executed over data stored in distributed storage systems like HDFS. Feature engineering with Hive involves writing SQL scripts to clean, aggregate, and transform data. While Hive queries are not as performant as Spark due to their reliance on MapReduce, they offer a familiar interface for analysts transitioning from traditional relational databases to big data environments. For organizations that already have large Hive warehouses, integrating Hive-based feature engineering into modern pipelines via tools like Apache Livy or Presto can bridge the gap between old and new systems.

Google BigQuery and Amazon Redshift offer cloud-native alternatives for scalable feature engineering. These platforms provide fully managed data warehouses that support SQL queries over petabyte-scale datasets. In these environments, feature engineering is often expressed as SQL views or stored procedures that preprocess raw data into model-ready tables. BigQuery's support for user-defined functions and window functions enables sophisticated transformations such as calculating user-level statistics, identifying sequential patterns, and performing cohort analysis. Because these services are serverless and automatically scale with data size, they remove much of the operational complexity associated with infrastructure management, allowing teams to focus more on the feature logic itself.

In addition to these platforms, feature engineering at scale often benefits from dedicated orchestration and workflow management tools. Apache Airflow, for example, is widely used to schedule and monitor complex data pipelines, ensuring that dependencies are respected and that feature generation jobs run reliably at the required intervals. Airflow's DAGs (Directed Acyclic Graphs) define the flow of data transformations from raw inputs to final feature sets. Combined with containerization technologies like Docker and orchestration systems like Kubernetes, these tools help ensure that large-scale feature engineering jobs are reproducible, isolated, and fault-tolerant.

Another critical component of scalable feature engineering is the storage and access pattern for features. At large scales, simply calculating features is not enough—they must be stored in a way that allows fast and consistent access by downstream consumers, including machine learning models. Distributed key-value stores such as Redis, Cassandra, or HBase are often used for this purpose. These systems allow precomputed features to be served at low latency to real-time applications. When integrated with a feature store, they enable teams to manage feature definitions, track feature versions, and ensure consistent behavior across environments. This layer abstracts the complexity of distributed systems while enforcing best practices such as schema enforcement, freshness guarantees, and access control.

Scalable feature engineering also involves optimizing computational efficiency. This includes minimizing data shuffling, leveraging partitioning and bucketing strategies, avoiding wide joins, and using vectorized operations whenever possible. Understanding the execution plan of distributed queries is essential for identifying bottlenecks and improving pipeline performance. Engineers must work closely with platform-specific monitoring tools and logs to diagnose slow stages, memory pressure, or network overhead. Writing efficient code in big data systems often means thinking in terms of distributed systems theory, where the cost of communication, serialization, and fault recovery can far exceed the cost of computation.

Data quality assurance is another pillar of scalable feature engineering. At massive scale, even a small percentage of bad data can lead to misleading features and degraded model performance. Automated validation checks must be integrated into the feature pipelines to detect anomalies such as null values, unexpected cardinality, or skewed distributions. Tools like Great Expectations or Deequ allow for declarative data quality tests that can be embedded in big data workflows. These tests help maintain trust in the features and serve as early warnings for upstream data issues or changes in data semantics.

Scalable feature engineering with big data tools is not just about using powerful technologies—it is about designing systems that are efficient, consistent, and resilient. It requires a multidisciplinary approach that blends data science, software engineering, and distributed systems knowledge. By leveraging platforms such as Spark, Beam, BigQuery, and Airflow, teams can build feature pipelines that scale with data growth, adapt to evolving business needs, and deliver robust inputs to machine learning models. As data volumes continue to expand and real-time applications become the norm, the ability to engineer features at scale will remain a core capability for any organization pursuing advanced analytics and artificial intelligence.

Continuous Tuning and Monitoring in Production

Continuous tuning and monitoring in production are essential practices for maintaining the reliability, accuracy, and efficiency of machine learning models once they are deployed. While much attention is given to model development and initial deployment, real-world systems do not exist in static environments. Data distributions shift, user behavior evolves, infrastructure changes, and external conditions fluctuate. These factors can cause even well-performing models to degrade over time if left unchecked. Therefore, machine learning systems must be actively managed post-deployment through processes that continuously evaluate performance, detect anomalies, trigger alerts, and recommend or apply updates. This lifecycle-oriented approach is what differentiates mature machine learning operations from isolated experimentation.

The need for continuous tuning begins with the recognition that model parameters and hyperparameters optimized during training may no longer be optimal once the model is exposed to live data. What works well during cross-validation might fail under different operational constraints such as latency, throughput, or memory limits. Moreover, the statistical properties of incoming data can drift gradually or abruptly, affecting the relevance of features and the accuracy of predictions. Continuous tuning involves revisiting hyperparameters, retraining with new data, adjusting learning rates, reweighting loss functions, or even replacing the underlying model architecture when necessary. These changes must be made systematically, with proper evaluation and rollback mechanisms in place to avoid destabilizing production systems.

Effective monitoring is the foundation of continuous tuning. Monitoring begins with tracking prediction performance over time using key metrics such as accuracy, precision, recall, F1 score, AUC, and mean squared error, depending on the problem type. These metrics must be calculated not just overall but also segmented by time, user group, geographic region, or other relevant dimensions to detect localized issues. Monitoring systems should compare current performance against historical baselines, triggering alerts when deviations exceed acceptable thresholds. For classification models, tracking the confusion matrix over time can reveal changes in misclassification patterns, while for regression models, residual analysis can highlight increasing error variance or bias.

Beyond traditional performance metrics, monitoring must extend to data quality and data drift. Input features should be monitored for missing values, unexpected formats, extreme values, and changes in distribution. Data drift occurs when the statistical properties of input variables change over time, while concept drift happens when the relationship between inputs and outputs evolves. Both types of drift can erode model accuracy. Tools such as Population Stability Index, Kolmogorov-Smirnov tests, and Kullback-Leibler divergence help quantify drift, while visualizations such as histograms, time series plots, and heatmaps make drift interpretable for human review. Monitoring systems should log these metrics and surface them through dashboards or automated reports that enable rapid diagnostics.

Anomalies in model behavior often signal deeper issues. For example, a sudden spike in prediction latency might indicate infrastructure problems, increased data volume, or inefficient feature processing. A drop in prediction confidence could result from noisy inputs, schema changes, or unrecognized categories. An increase in prediction variance may suggest that the model is encountering inputs unlike those it saw during training. Monitoring must cover not only model outputs but also system-level metrics such as CPU utilization, memory consumption, API response times, and error rates. Correlating model metrics with system metrics can help distinguish between data-related issues and infrastructure bottlenecks.

Automated retraining is one of the most common responses to performance degradation in production. This process involves scheduling model retraining jobs at regular intervals or triggering them in response to monitored signals such as drift detection, performance decay, or data accumulation. Retraining pipelines should incorporate data preprocessing, feature extraction, hyperparameter tuning, validation, and deployment steps. These pipelines must be reproducible, version-controlled, and resilient to data anomalies. Before deploying a retrained model, it is critical to compare its performance against the current model using A/B testing, shadow deployment, or canary releases. This ensures that the update brings tangible improvements and does not introduce regressions.

Hyperparameter tuning in production environments requires special consideration. Unlike in development, where exhaustive grid or random search can be performed over long durations, production tuning must be efficient and guided by real-world constraints. Bayesian optimization, bandit algorithms, or meta-learning approaches can be employed to explore the hyperparameter space intelligently. These methods prioritize configurations that are likely to improve performance while limiting experimentation overhead. In latency-sensitive applications, tuning may also involve trade-offs between model complexity and inference speed. Techniques such as model pruning, quantization, and distillation may be applied to strike the right balance between accuracy and efficiency.

Monitoring must also extend to fairness, explainability, and compliance. As machine learning models influence critical decisions, it is essential to ensure that they do not exhibit unintended bias or discrimination. Continuous fairness audits involve tracking metrics such as demographic parity, equal opportunity, and disparate impact across protected groups. Explainability tools like SHAP or LIME can be used to audit feature attributions and detect if the model's reasoning has shifted in undesirable ways. In regulated industries, monitoring must also ensure compliance with legal standards and internal governance policies, including data retention rules, audit logging, and access controls.

A crucial component of continuous tuning and monitoring is feedback integration. Models should not operate in isolation from the systems and people they serve. Feedback from users, domain experts, or downstream systems provides valuable signals for identifying blind spots, correcting errors, and prioritizing improvements. Feedback loops can be manual, such as labeling incorrect predictions, or automated, such as click-through rates, conversions, or human-in-the-loop annotations. Incorporating this feedback into the retraining process allows models to evolve in response to real-world behavior, increasing their relevance and utility.

Documentation and transparency are vital for operational excellence. Every tuning decision, retraining event, and detected anomaly should be logged with contextual information. Versioning of models, data, and features ensures that changes can be traced and audited. Observability platforms should provide visibility into the full lineage of predictions, from raw input to final output, including feature values, transformations, model parameters, and intermediate steps. This level of traceability is necessary not only for debugging but also for building trust with stakeholders and satisfying regulatory requirements.

In mature machine learning operations, continuous tuning and monitoring are not afterthoughts but integral parts of the development cycle. They transform models from static artifacts into living systems that adapt to changing environments, respond to feedback, and remain aligned with business objectives. Achieving this level of operational maturity requires collaboration between data scientists, engineers, DevOps teams, and product managers. It demands robust infrastructure, clear processes, and a culture that prioritizes reliability and accountability. As machine learning continues to power an increasing number of products and services, continuous tuning and monitoring will define the line between experimental prototypes and production-grade intelligence.